# A
# COLLECTOR'S
# COLLECTION

# A COLLECTOR'S COLLECTION

## Humorous & Uplifting Stories
### TOLD BY ONE OF TODAY'S
## Top Fund-Raisers

## RABBI
# ChaimOrange

JERUSALEM
PUBLICATIONS

Jerusalem

First published 2004

ISBN 0-9761862-0-9

Copyright © 2004 by JERUSALEM PUBLICATIONS

Distributed by Feldheim Publishers
208 Airport Executive Park,
Nanuet, NY 10954
1-800-237-7149


JERUSALEM PUBLICATIONS
Jerusalem, Israel


10 9 8 7 6 5 4 3

*Printed in Israel*

לז"נ הרב חיים בן משה יוסף זצ"ל

# SCHMELCZER

*Rosh Yeshiva of*
*Telshe Yeshiva-Chicago*
*Ambassador for G-d, Torah and Klal Yisrael*

תנצב"ה

Rabbi CHAIM P. SCHEINBERG

Rosh Hayeshiva "TORAH ORE"

and Morah Hora'ah of Kiryat Mattersdorf

הרב חיים פינחס שיינברג

ראש ישיבת "תורה אור"

ומורה הוראה דקרית מטרסדורף

Rabbi Chaim Orange, who for thirty-five years has devoted himself to fund-raising for our Yeshiva, is now putting out a collection of stories that highlight the work of those who toil far from
home to raise the funds that allow the fire of Torah to burn.

The benefit a person gains from giving tzedaka is greater than
most people realize. The Vilna Gaon, *ztz"l*, says on the *passuk* in
*Mishlei* (10:2) וצדקה תציל ממות, "*Tzedaka* saves from death":
אבל צדקה לא די שהוא טוב בעצם אלא גם מועיל יותר מכל דבר שמציל
אף ממות ואין מועיל בעולם יותר מזה, "Not only is *tzedaka* good
itself, but it is more effective than anything else because it saves
even from death. And there is nothing more effective in the
world than this."

I would like to give my *beracha* that the *zechus* of Torah protect
Rav Chaim and all those who support Torah, and may they see
much *nachas* and *beracha* in their lives and in the lives of their
families.

בברכת התורה,

**GRAND RABBI MOSHE SAKS**

**CHIEF RABBI**

of the "KEHILAS HAYEREIM"
ORTHODOX RABBINICAL COURT
RABBI of ROMEMA
for the ORTHODOX COMMUNITY
(KIRYAT MATTESDORF)
•
14  PANIM MEYROT ST., JERUSALEM TEL. 02-5372127

משה סאקם

ראב"ד

בד"ץ קהילת היראים
רב רומ"ץ שכונת רוממה והסביבה החרדית
מח"ס "מתנת משה" שו"ת, על הש"ס, עה"ח
בעיה"ק ירושלים ת"ו
•
רח' פנים מאירות 14 ירושלים טל: 02-5372127

בעזה"י ___ ב' אלול תשס"ז

There are two conceptions of charity. One is: וצדקה תהיה
לנו כי נשמר לעשות את כל המצוה הזות... (*Devarim* 6:25). This
refers to the tzedaka a person does for his own soul. By
keeping the mitzvos, he does the greatest charity, for his
soul will not be blackened, but instead will have the world
to come for eternity, and he will receive his charity from
Hashem Yisborach מידה כנגד מידה.

Then there is the second charity, the giving of funds to help
the poor, etc., and helping Torah learning and *yiras
Shomayim*, etc.

Rabbi Chaim Orange has harvested a collection of unique
stories that combine both charities, because he shows the
Divine hand of Hashem Yisborach — how in hundreds of
cases the physical and material help and the money people
gave led those same people to begin to serve the Almighty
and helped them to give charity to their own souls by keeping the holy Torah. You can actually see *hashgacha* and
*siyatta diShemaya*. This alone is also a charity, as it says,
והאמין בד' ויחשב' לו.

May this book bring a deeper understanding of the
solicitators who come, and may it help us to appreciate them, because they help us attain great rewards
in both worlds. We wish Rabbi Orange success that
the book find wide acceptance by the public and
bring the author *hatzlacha* and all the best.

*Sincerely,*
*Rabbi Moshe Saks*

OHR SOMAYACH אור שמח
TANENBAUM COLLEGE

September 2, 2004
ט"ז אלול תשס"ד

Rabbi Chaim Orange is one of the warmest and funniest fundraisers in the world. Friends and neighbors like myself have been both inspired and amused for years by his stories of what a collector for a worthy cause faces while he is on the road performing his sacred mission.

Now this classical collector has collected contemporary and historical stories which he tells in his inimitable stream-of-consciousness style. These stories and the insights which accompany them will sometimes make you laugh and sometimes cry. But they will surely make you have a deeper understanding and appreciation of the challenges faced by those idealistic individuals who enable institutions and organizations to pay their bills and who serve as ambassadors of Torah to the people whose support they seek.

I have had the privilege of knowing Chaim and the outstanding yeshiva which he represents for a long time, and it is my hope that this book will offer you a chance to get to know him as well.

And if Chaim knocks at your door — let him in, guaranteed that you'll have as memorable an experience as you have had from reading his book.

Rabbi Mendel Weinbach
Rosh Hayeshiva
Yeshivat Ohr Somayach

Jerusalem          20th of Elul 5764

Rabbi Chaim Orange has been a dear friend and neighbor of mine for over thirty years. He is one of a kind — a unique blend of love for Torah, love of *chesed*, cheerfulness, and humor.

Reb Chaim's colorful personality comes through in this book, which is informative, inspiring, interesting, and entertaining.

As a student of the great Torah scholar and tzaddik, Rabbi Chaim Pinchos Scheinberg, *shlita*, he is clear in his goal to help support Yeshiva Torah Ore, and this clarity gives him the inner strength and fortitude to say and do what many would find difficult. Seeing the eternal value of Torah and *chesed* from the perspective of his Rebbe, transforms the challenges everyone in his profession will face into a tremendous privilege. It gives one the opportunity to help others accomplish for Torah.

I'm certain there will be people who will contact Rabbi Orange to visit them when he is in their city so they can watch him in action. Besides the mitzvah of their donation, they will have a memorable experience. Don't be surprised if you will see would-be fund-raisers following Reb Chaim around to learn from his many years of experience. This book is the next best thing to having him serve as a mentor.

After reading this book, you will view the entire process of raising money for worthy causes and institutions in a broader, more comprehensive way. You will gain a greater understanding of what it means to be a fund-raiser. Be prepared to find yourself giving tzedaka with more heart and soul.

*Zelig Pliskin*

Zelig Pliskin

# Contents

# Preface

**I'm not a writer.** In fact, I hate to write, and I usually put off any writing I have to do as much as possible. However, since no one has ever written a book about fund-raising, or, as it is better known in the Jewish vernacular, schnorring, I felt that as someone in the business for decades, I should do it. My basic reasons for doing so are to clear up common misconceptions and to show you the other side of the fund-raising coin (pun intended).

Many *baalebatim* think fund-raisers are (a) simpletons who cannot get any other decent job, (b) too lazy to hold down a steady job, (c) thieves who enjoy ripping off people, (d) frauds looking for the easy money that can be made off the gullible public, (e) freeloaders eager for a free trip to the States. I hope you'll have a different picture after you've read the stories in this book.

What makes this business different from all others is that a fund-raiser not only represents the *rosh yeshiva* or *rosh kollel* plus the entire faculty, student body and staff of his institution — in my case Yeshivas Torah Ore — but even more important, he represents G–d.

I am always asked if I enjoy fund-raising. The answer is obvious. Would you enjoy a job where the door is slammed shut in your face? Yes, it's happened to me. So why do it?

The easiest explanation, to my way of thinking, is that more than a way to make an honest living, fund-raising is the best way for me to ensure a good portion in the next world not only for myself, but for my wife, and for my children, who, unfortunately, have to be fatherless several months of the year. I hope that my running around for Torah will bring merit to them, their children and future generations. As Rav Yisrael Salanter used to say: "If someone goes out collecting for a charitable cause, he can't help but be successful. If people give, he gets money. And if they don't, he gets something worth more than money."

Many of the stories and anecdotes in this book happened to me, some to my friends in the business and others were told to me. I have also included hand-picked stories, each a gem, to show how *gedolim* in recent times and in previous eras viewed the give and the take of *tzedaka*.

# Acknowledgments

**First and foremost,** I'd like to give thanks to G-d for enabling me to finish this book. If this work helps people to open their hearts and their pockets to give or to give more, then all the work was worth it.

I would also like to give special thanks to my wife, who stood by me all these many long years of fund-raising to support Torah, and who even managed to find the time to type the entire original manuscript of this book.

Many thanks to Rabbi and Mrs. Binyamin Dinnovitz, who helped me get started on the road to fund-raising.

Special thanks to all the people who have opened their homes not only to me but to all the other *meshulachim*, and to the people who have come to the aid of Yeshiva Torah Ore, thereby making my job that much easier.

May this book be an *aliya* for the *neshamos* of my parents and my father-in-law, may they rest in peace, and a *zechus* for, *tlct"a*, my mother-in-law Mrs. Shula Zukowsky. May it also be an *aliya* for the *neshama* of Yisroel ben Pesach Yosef, *a"h*, who in his own small way did a lot for *Yiddishkeit*, and a *zechus* for, *tlct"a*, Faige Basya *bas* Yenta.

May this book be a *zechus* for my children Yisroel Meir and Yoela Orange and family; Zalman Aryeh Menachem and Miriam Orange and family; Tuvia and Rena Elka Pollack and family; Mordechai, Miriam Leiba, Moshe, Elisheva, and last but not least, Chana Bracha.

Special thanks to Rabbi Hillel Cooperman for letting me use some of his material from the book *Me'il Tzedaka*.

Thanks to:

Mr. Rachmiel Daykin, for translating source material from *lashon kodesh*.

Mrs. Yehudis Golshevsky, for her extensive editing of the original stories.

Reb Shlomo Zalman Rappaport of JERUSALEM PUBLICATIONS, for believing in the book from the beginning and for not giving up on me until it was finished. To members of his team: thanks to Mrs. Debby Ismailoff for her careful proofreading of the book; *yashar koach* to Mr. David Yaphe for giving me the cover I wanted, and to the senior editor at JERUSALEM PUBLICATIONS for giving me the book I wanted.

Special thanks as well to the distinguished people who have read, commented and given constructive criticism on this book.

# Persistence Pays

The Ponovezher Rav went to see a *baal habayis* for a donation. When the *baal habayis* wrote out a check for ten thousand dollars, the rav said he had come for much more serious money.

The *baal habayis* was considered to be wealthy even among the wealthy, and so he wrote a check for one hundred thousand dollars.

The rav knew with whom he was dealing, so before cashing the check, he walked into the man's bank and asked the teller if there was enough money in the account to cover the check.

"I'm sorry," said the teller, "but there's only $87,000 in the account."

On the spot, the Ponovezher Rav made a deposit of just over $13,000 and then cashed the $100,000 check.

# Persistence Pays

**F**und-raising is a full-time job to which you must devote all your time and energy if you really want to succeed — and no matter what people say, you can succeed. It's not easy, but it can be done. To succeed at fund-raising, you have to persist. A good fund-raiser will use every means at his disposal to get people to give, including some never thought of before.

For instance, there once was a fund-raiser who always walked the streets of a certain neighborhood carrying a broomstick. Understandably, everyone who saw him walking around that way thought he had a problem. Finally, one person asked why he did it. The fund-raiser answered, "In the wealthier neighborhoods, many homes are surrounded by gates that are always locked. The only way to ring the doorbell is by pushing the broomstick through the bars!"

**A fund-raiser also needs** to have the brains and the nerve to say the right thing to the right person at the right time. Irving M. Bunim, the famous American philanthropist, was forever trying to get an appointment with a wealthy businessman so that he could solicit a donation from him. Every time he called, the man's secretary refused to put her boss on the line. When Mr. Bunim went to the office, he couldn't get past her desk. Finally, he hit upon a novel idea. He called and asked the secretary to please inform her boss that a mutual relative had died and left an important legacy.

"Tell your employer to please return my call as soon as possible," he said.

Barely fifteen minutes passed before Mr. Bunim's telephone rang. The boss was on the line, wanting to know details.

Mr. Bunim's reply? "Our mutual relative is Moshe Rabbeinu, and the legacy is the holy Torah."

The ruse worked, and the man gave a generous donation.

**Back in the old days** of the Chofetz Chaim Yeshiva in Williamsburg, the *rosh yeshiva*, Rabbi Henoch Leibowitz, would send the boys out to raise funds when money was tight. One student in particular was a real go-getter. While passing through a major midwestern city, he decided to try to solicit a donation from the owner of a shoe company, a man known never to give a penny to any institution whatsoever.

The young man confidently strode into the office, walked straight up to the secretary's desk and asked to see the boss.

"What company do you represent?" she asked.

Pulling out his all-purpose card that announced him simply as "Rabbi So-and-so," he suavely told the secretary that he was the salesman for the "Heavenly Shoe Company."

As soon as he was shown into the executive office, the game was up. The boss pounced on him, shouting, "What kind of chutzpa is it for a rabbi to come and impersonate a shoe salesman!" He pointed to the card, growing more and more furious with each passing second.

The quick-witted young man was ready with his response.

"Sir, I do indeed represent the Heavenly Shoe Company. If you donate money to the Chofetz Chaim Yeshiva in New York, I promise to testify on your behalf upstairs when your time comes. In the merit of giving charity, you will walk to heaven in your heavenly shoes!"

The young rabbi got his donation, and he was the only person who ever did get money out of the man!

**This next story shows** just what you can do with a single, well-chosen word.

A fund-raiser once tried to get in to see a wealthy man named Reb Asher, but by the time he got to his house, a whole roomful of people was already waiting. The man's personal assistant told the fund-raiser he would have to come back another day.

Since this fund-raiser was pressed for time, he promised that if he was admitted, he would say only one word.

Seeing that he was serious, the assistant let him in.

When the fund-raiser entered the rich man's private room, Reb Asher asked him what he wanted.

The fund-raiser cryptically responded with one word: "Gemara."

"Just what is that supposed to mean?" Reb Asher asked.

The fund-raiser smiled and said, "It stands for 'Good Morning, Reb Asher.'" Then, without missing a beat, he repeated the word: "Gemara."

Amused, Reb Asher played along. "What does it mean now?"

This time the fund-raiser answered, "**Give Me, Reb A**sher."

Reb Asher good-naturedly handed him a donation, but the fund-raiser didn't budge. Instead, he repeated for the third time, "Gemara."

By now, Reb Asher was getting impatient, but his curiosity made him ask, "What does it mean this time?"

With a smile, the fund-raiser said, "**Give More, Reb A**sher!"

**Instead of walking away** from a challenge, a good fund-raiser meets it head-on. Rabbi Moshe Aharon Stern once went to see a prosperous businessman for a donation. When he walked into the office, the businessman told him that he didn't want to hear about yeshivos.

"Then what are you interested in talking about?" asked Rabbi Stern.

"Baseball," the man shot back.

Not one to be put off that easily when it came to raising funds for Torah, Rabbi Stern answered, "I'm not up-to-date on today's baseball, but let me tell you about the '29 Yankees."

Half an hour later, he walked out with a nice-sized check.

**Every so often,** I meet up with a *baal habayis* who furnishes me with every imaginable reason as to why he just can't give me any money. This happens to every fund-raiser at some time or another. Though I usually tend to take such refusals at face value and move on, there are times when a different approach is needed.

Once a *baal habayis* told me that he was sorry, but he couldn't give me a penny because all his *maaser* money was being used by his uncle, a *talmid chacham* who needed funds to print his *sefarim*.

I immediately said, "If you don't want to support our

yeshiva, that's fine. But I won't stand here and listen to you slander yourself!"

"Rabbi, what are you talking about?"

"First of all," I said, "I'm sure that you support the yeshiva where you learned and the yeshivos where your kids are learning. Second, a successful businessman like you would never have a portfolio containing only one stock. You would diversify to protect yourself in case another company proves stronger than the first.

"It's the same with yeshivos," I continued. "You'd be sure to get a piece of the action of every institution, if only to be on the safe side."

I walked out of there with a substantial sum.

**A fund-raiser once came to see** a *baal habayis*, but even though he had been admitted, the *baal habayis* kept on saying the same thing: "I'm sorry, I'm very busy. I don't have any time. But please come back when I'm not busy."

Despite this, the fund-raiser refused to give up. Every time he left, he would say, "I'll come again some other time. Be well. I only wish I had another hundred people like you."

At long last, the fund-raiser managed to catch the *baal habayis* when he had a spare moment. He gave his spiel, and the *baal habayis* gave him a generous donation, apologizing all the while. "I'm sorry to have made you come back so many times. But one thing never made sense."

"Oh? What's that?"

The *baal habayis* went on. "When I kept on sending you away, why did you always say that you wished you had another hundred people like me?"

"Because I already have another thousand people like you!"

**Rabbi Moshe Schwab** once went to a person's home to get a donation. When the person answered the door, he refused to give the rabbi a donation. Not only that, but he slammed the door in his face.

Rabbi Schwab went straight to the nearest phone booth and called back this person.

"If you don't want to give me a donation, that's one thing, but you don't have the right to slam the door in my face. Good-bye."

This person later ended up giving Rabbi Schwab a large donation.

**Rabbi Rosen** once went to a fund-raising dinner, and while he was there, he ran into his real estate lawyer.

The lawyer said to the rabbi, "There's someone here in this room I think might want to help your yeshiva. He's over there, up front."

The lawyer walked the rabbi over to the acquaintance and introduced him as Shimon. Shimon promptly gave the rabbi his phone number and suggested he call him in the morning.

When Rabbi Rosen called Shimon's office at nine thirty the next morning, the secretary said that her boss was out on a delivery and told him to call back at twelve thirty.

Rabbi Rosen didn't manage to call back at the appointed time, but he tried again later in the day, only to be told that the boss was out on another delivery. This went on for several days.

Rabbi Rosen was at a loss. *Why on earth did my lawyer introduce me to this guy?* he asked himself. *If he has money, he ought to have someone else making the deliveries for him. And if he's running around doing deliveries, he can't have too much money!*

After days of frustration, the rabbi blurted out to the secretary, "If he's the one who's out making deliveries all day, what kind of businessman is he?"

The secretary said wryly, "Sir, he's an obstetrician."

**One of the hardest times** for a fund-raiser is what I call "the twilight hour." That is the time of day when most people are closing up their shops or offices and getting ready to commute home to their families and dinner. That stretch of time is not the best time to see a potential donor.

During these two hours of wasted time, all a fund-raiser can do is twiddle his thumbs, waiting on pins and needles until he can hit the road again.

One day, instead of wasting time, a fund-raiser friend of mine decided to give a certain *baal habayis* a try.

"What have I got to lose?" he reasoned.

To his surprise, he was welcomed into the man's office and given a nice donation.


**In addition to persistence**, quick wits are an advantage in fund-raising. Once, an elderly man who had learned in Novarodok came to raise funds in one of the European capitals. Since it is always easier to circulate in pairs, he found a young man who was willing to go along with him.

They arrived at a certain multimillionaire's palatial estate, which had marble columns adorning the entrance. As they passed between two columns, the elderly fund-raiser spat right at one of them.

The young man was taken aback, but thought, *That's strange, but maybe his mouth was full of phlegm, and he wanted to clear it out before going in to speak to the baal habayis.*

Before the young man even finished the thought, his elderly partner thundered, "Money should be used to support Torah, not to advertise wealth! Otherwise, money is meaningless."

And this was before they even rang the bell!

"I learned this from my rabbis in Novarodok," he glowered.

They rang the bell and were ushered into the house by a servant. Standing before them were a few sculptures on pedestals.

The elderly man removed his hat and hung it on the first. He then took off his overcoat and draped it over the second.

The *baal habayis* showed the two men into his study. The walls were covered with priceless artwork. The elderly rabbi went over to each painting and turned it to face the wall.

Exasperated, the *baal habayis* went over to the young man and asked, "What do I have to do to stop this person from turning my house inside out?"

The young man cleverly answered, "If you'll just give him the money he came for, he will thank you kindly and be on his way."

And that's exactly what happened.


**How's this one** for quick thinking? An extremely wealthy business magnate in North America was sued in court and, for the first time, lost the case. When journalists asked for his reaction, he was quoted as saying, "It was a small pittance."

The very next morning, someone knocked on the wealthy man's front door. When the door was opened, standing there was a very famous fund-raiser. When he was asked what he wanted, the fund-raiser said, "The yeshiva I represent needs money, and I've come to get a small pittance."


**Whenever I'm running around** covering my route, I always try to expand on the number of people that I see. Naturally, I also always try to improve on the amount of money that people give. Once I knocked on a door that I had never come to before, and got a great shock. From the other side of the door, I could hear the deep growl and loud barking of an enormous dog. I know people own pets, but from the sound of it, this animal was this size of a young colt!

I was faced with a choice. I could either turn right around and leave as fast as possible, or hold my ground and hope for the best. I opted for the latter, and prayed that the beast wouldn't be able to sneak out the door.

At long last, the woman of the house came to see what the racket was about and asked who I was. I told her my name and the name of my yeshiva.

She said, "Wait right here. I'm going to put the dog in the other room."

When she returned, I entered the house.

"You know," she told me, "the dog is really harmless, but when other fund-raisers hear his bark, they just take off."

In other words, I was one of very few fund-raisers that had actually entered her home, and she considered me quite brave for not running away. She then told me that it was her mother's *yahrtzeit*, and that she always made sure to give a certain amount of money to *tzedaka* on this day.

"From now on, you'll be the lucky recipient. I'll set the money aside for you each year."

**Some of my favorite stories** are about how our Torah greats used their genius to outsmart donors and get more money for *tzedaka*.

Once, a donor gave the Satmar Rav, Rabbi Yoel Teitelbaum, forty-seven dollars. When the Rebbe asked him how he had come up with that figure, the would-be donor said that it was the *gematria* of the Rebbe's name, Yoel.

"If that's the case," countered the Rebbe, "you can call me Yoelish." (The *gematria* of "Yoelish," the name by which the Rebbe was affectionately known, equals 357.)

**Rav Kahaneman**, the Ponovezher Rav, was a master fund-raiser. He once went to a wealthy *baal habayis* to ask for a donation. This man told the Rav that he would be willing to part with thousands of dollars, provided that the Rav would open a school where none of the students would ever wear a yarmulke or tzitzis. Here was a golden opportunity — but how could he possibly comply with these terms?

The *rosh yeshiva* finally acquiesced.

What did he do? He opened a girls' school that is flourishing to this day!

**On another occasion**, a *baal habayis* told the Ponovezher Rav that he would donate a princely sum to the famous Ponovezher Yeshiva — provided that the rav hang his portrait on the wall of the *beis medrash*.

How could he get around this one?

True to form, the rav quickly thought of a solution.

"Anyone," he told the would-be donor, "can get his picture put up in the *beis medrash*. Someone of your stature, though, deserves a more dignified location. Your picture should hang in my office, where only the most distinguished people enter."

Naturally, the *baal habayis* was thrilled to be so honored, and the rav collected the check.

**A certain rabbi**, whom we'll call Rabbi Bloom, had a knack for figuring out different schemes for raising money for his yeshiva. One brainstorm was the time he hung out a sign on his building saying something to the effect of "Curing Cancer the Torah Way."

The Weizmann Institute of Science in Rechovot also had a research project into curing cancer at the time. When the professor in charge of the program at the Weizmann Institute heard about the sign affixed to the yeshiva's building, he called the *rosh yeshiva* and told him point-blank that it was bringing negative publicity to the institute. If the *rosh yeshiva* stopped, the professor would give him in exchange a full doctorate from the Weizmann Institute, which meant that he, the *rosh yeshiva*, could give a doctorate to anyone else.

The *rosh yeshiva* consented, because he had other ways of making money.

Later, his son-in-law asked him for a doctorate, and he got it.

Now when he goes to see people and he has to get through the secretary, he just hands over his card that says doctor on it. For all the secretary knows, the boss may be having heart problems, so the "doctor" usually gets in right away.

**Rav Meir Shapiro of Lublin** is another *rosh yeshiva* famed for his fund-raising abilities. Once he asked a certain *gevir* to come and see him. The *gevir* knew what the *rosh yeshiva* was after, so he begged off, claming to be ill.

Rav Shapiro lowered himself to go to the home of the *gevir*, where he saw the man sitting at his table, hale and hearty.

"I think," said Rav Shapiro with a twinkle in his eye, "I'm a pretty good doctor. You seem to have recovered completely after only one visit. The least you can do is to pay me for my services!"

**When Rav Chaim Soloveitchik** was the rav in Brisk, he once sent for a wealthy but miserly man. The man came, and Reb Chaim brought him into a private room where he told him why he had brought him, as well as how much he wanted.

"But Rabbi," the miser protested, "I can't give that much!"

Reb Chaim stood up and said, "Wait here for an hour until I return," and he walked out.

The *gevir* waited the hour, and when Reb Chaim didn't return, he decided to leave. To his dismay, he found that the door was locked from the outside.

Shortly afterward, Reb Chaim returned. "Don't be angry that I took so long," he said. "I saw that you're a hard man to persuade, and I just don't have the time to waste. People need me, and that's why I left you here by yourself to think the matter over."

The *gevir* relented and gave Reb Chaim the amount he had asked for.

**Another time** when Reb Chaim wanted to get a donation from a wealthy man known to be stingy, he sent for the man.

When the *gevir* came and heard why he had been called, he was annoyed.

"When a person needs someone to do him a favor," he complained, "he doesn't usually call that person to come to him! He's the one who should go."

"I thought my trip would be a waste of time, so I didn't go to you," said Reb Chaim.

"So?" the miser retorted. "You took care of yourself, but what about wasting my time?"

"That," answered Reb Chaim, "is something you can still rectify!"

**Rabbi Naftali Tzvi Yehuda Berlin**, the Netziv, *rosh yeshiva* of Volozhin Yeshiva, once came to a certain city to raise money for his yeshiva. In that town, there lived a man who had a hard time parting with his money. He wanted to give, but not an amount that was on a par with his financial standing. The Netziv told him that it was wrong for him to make the community into a bunch of liars.

"How am I doing that?" asked the miser.

"Simple," answered the Netziv. "Everyone, for example, calls me 'Harav Hagaon,' so I do whatever I can to live up to my name. I answer halachic queries, I write books on Torah, I have a yeshiva, and I teach Torah — all this so that there will be at least some semblance of the truth to what people say about me.

By the same token, a rich man should be the first one to give a hefty contribution. But you don't, so you're making the community into a bunch of liars!"

**Rabbi Shalom of Kaminka** once came to a wealthy man for a donation. The rich man put off his request by saying, "I have poor people in my own family."

"Why don't you finish the sentence?" Rabbi Shalom asked him.

"What do you mean?" wondered the *gevir*.

Rabbi Shalom smiled and said, "...and if I don't give to them, why on earth should I give to anyone else?"

**Speaking of relatives**, Rabbi Menachem Dovid of Amshinov once came to a wealthy man to raise money for the man's own kin.

"What does he have to do with me?" the *gevir* retorted. "He's a distant relative."

"Excuse me," asked Rabbi Menachem Dovid, "but do you pray every day?"

"What do you mean? Of course I pray every day!"

"What's the first blessing of the Shemoneh Esrei?" asked the rabbi.

"Even a cheder boy knows that one: 'G-d of Avraham, G-d of Yitzchak, and G-d of Yaakov.'"

Rabbi Menachem Dovid went on. "Who were Avraham, Yitzchak, and Yaakov?"

Getting impatient, the rich man muttered, "Our forefathers."

The rabbi pressed on. "When did they live?"

"A few thousand years ago."

"Interesting," mused the rabbi. "You have no trouble bringing up three times a day your relationship with distant relatives who lived a few thousand years ago to ask for G-d's help in their merit. Yet you don't want to remember your own distant relative who is alive right now!"

**Reb Yechezkel of Plonsk**, *Hy"d*, once went to a *gevir* to ask for a donation. The man refused and didn't give anything, but as the conversation went on, the *baal habayis* mentioned that he was a direct descendant of the Magen Avraham.

"I'm not so sure," said Reb Yechezkel.

"What do you mean by that?" asked the *gevir*.

"You never find a *Magen Avraham* without a *Machatzis Hashekel*." (This is a play on words. The literal meaning of *machatzis hashekel*, which is a standard commentary on the *Magen Avraham*, is "half a shekel.")

**Rabbi Mordechai Benet**, chief rabbi of Moravia in the early nineteenth century, once went to a very rich, miserly and sinful man, to ask for a donation.

The rich man answered sweetly, "But rabbi, I like to give charity secretly. It's better to give secretly than openly, you know."

Rabbi Benet smiled and said, "It's interesting that when you sin secretly, the entire town knows about it. But when you give charity secretly, not a soul knows what you've been up to!"

**Rabbi Yitzchak of Vorki** once chastised one of his wealthy chassidim. The man was known to be really tightfisted, and Reb Yitzchak told him, "A man of your stature is obligated to eat meat and fish and to drink wine, not to live from Shabbos to Shabbos on stale bread and water!"

Later, Reb Yitzchak was asked why he had chastised his chassid in that fashion.

"Who cares what the man eats?" his chassidim asked.

Reb Yitzchak answered, "I really don't care what he eats. But if he eats stale bread and water all week long, what will he give to the poor? On the other hand, if he eats well all week long, then the poor at least can hope to get some stale bread out of him!"

**The Malbim** once went to pray in the synagogue of a certain town. While he was there, he saw the townspeople kissing the Torah scroll with their hands. When a poor person came in to ask for charity, however, they didn't give him a penny.

The Malbim said, "I see an upside-down world here in your synagogue. You kiss the Torah scroll with your hands, and give a donation with your mouths. You should be doing things the other way around: kiss the Torah with your mouths, and give money to the poor with your hands!"

**Once, Rabbi Meir Shapiro of Lublin** went to solicit funds from a *gevir* for the Chachmei Lublin Yeshiva. When the wealthy man saw Reb Meir coming, he got ready with a paltry donation.

"I'm sorry," said Reb Meir, "but I'm not a pregnant woman."

"What do you mean by that?" stammered the *gevir*.

"There are times when people give me honor, but they don't give me money. So I say, *Nu*, let it be a *kapara*. Other times, people give me money, but there's no *kavod haTorah*. So I say, Let it be a *kapara*. Here, I didn't get any honor or any money, so that makes two *kaparos*. And we all know that only a pregnant woman has to bring two *kaparos*!"

**"I learned how to raise money** from a fund-raiser," Rabbi Shapiro used to say. He once came to my door, and I handed him a silver zloty. He said, 'Give more, Rebbi.'

"I answered him, 'When someone gives you a groszy (a Polish penny), you accept it without saying a word. But when someone gives you a zloty, you argue. Why?'

"The fund-raiser explained his actions. 'When I get a groszy, and I argue with the person who gave it to me, all I wind up getting is another groszy. If I argue with the man who gave me a zloty, though, I might get another one!'"

Reb Meir would conclude, "I do exactly the same thing. When I go to a wealthy man, and he gives me a nice donation, I tell him the story of this fund-raiser."

**Once Rabbi Meir Shapira** traveled to America together with Reb Meir Dan of Ostrova to raise money for their respective institutions. During one of their conversations, Reb Meir Dan said to Reb Meir Shapira, "You must be the greater scholar, since you're able to raise more money that I am."

"On the contrary," answered Reb Meir Shapira, "You're more learned than I am, and that's why I'm able to raise more money than you are."

"How is that so?" asked Reb Meir Dan.

"I'll tell you a story to illustrate my point," said Reb Meir Shapira. "When I lived with my father-in-law, he used to lease bridges and hire tax collectors to guard them, so that he could collect taxes from all of the horses and carriages that crossed over. Once, he hired a Torah scholar to be the collector at one bridge, and a deaf simpleton to collect the tolls at the next bridge. At the Torah scholar's bridge, the same thing always happened: as people crossed over the bridge, the scholarly collector would get involved in a complex Torah topic. While he was so engrossed in his learning, all the horses and carriages would pass over the bridge without paying the toll.

"At the simpleton's bridge, however, the opposite was always the case. Whenever anyone tried to engage him in conversation, he would shout, 'What? I can't hear you! Tax for two horses is six pennies. Tax for one horse is three pence.' No matter what happened, he collected taxes from every traveler.

Talking to him was like talking to a wall.

"This is exactly our situation. When you go to see a *baal habayis*, you start to talk in learning. You tell him all about *Shas* and *poskim* until you forget what you've come for. In that way, the whole day can pass by without your managing to raise any money. As for me, when a *baal habayis* expresses an interest in talking about Torah, I make myself out to be a deaf man. I only know about one thing — money — and once I get it, I pick myself up and head straight for the next person."

**The Satmar Rav** once asked a man to give a donation. When the person asked, "Will the rav be happy if I give two times *chai*?" the Rebbe answered, "I'd be a lot happier if you'd give one times *meis*." (The *gematria* of *chai*, which means "life," is eighteen, whereas the *gematria* of *meis*, which means "dead," is 440.)

**Rabbi Meir Shapira** approached a wealthy man for a donation for Yeshivas Chachmei Lublin. The man refused him, saying, "Not me, not my children, and not my grandchildren will ever need yeshivos!"

Reb Meir exclaimed, "I'm astounded that anyone could be worse than Haman!"

"What is that supposed to mean?!" thundered the *gevir*.

"Well, we have a tradition that Haman's grandchildren learned in a yeshiva in Bnei Brak — yet you insist that it could never happen to any of your future descendants!"

The wealthy man immediately gave Reb Meir a generous donation.

**On a fund-raising trip** in America, Rabbi Meir Shapira once went to visit with a *gevir*. The rich man said, "Rabbi, why did you see fit to build such a large institution when expenses are so high and it's so hard to earn an income nowadays?

People are living in crushing poverty in Poland."

"I'll tell you a story," said Reb Meir. "Once a chassid went to his Rebbe to ask for advice. He wanted to buy stock, but he felt that it was risky — sometimes it shoots up, but sometimes it plummets.

"His Rebbe said, 'If you have wealthy people in your family on whom you can depend, then try it. But if not, then stay away from it.'

"We Jews in Poland have rich family in America on whom we can rely."

**Rav Shabsi Yudelevitch** asked the *gabbai* of the local shul to speak so that he could make an appeal for his yeshiva. The *gabbai* answered in the affirmative but when it came to it, he told Reb Shabsi he could speak for only three minutes.

Not one to be taken aback, Reb Shabsi approached the podium and began.

"A fire broke out, and Gan Eden said Gehinnom should pay, while Gehinnom claimed Gan Eden was to blame. Each group had its own team of lawyers. After much back and forth discussion, they finally came to a decision."

At this point, just as Reb Shabsi was about to say who won the case, he looked at his watch and walked away from the podium.

Everyone wanted to know the final decision, and people crowded around him in the shul.

"I'm sorry," he said. "The *gabbai* gave me only three minutes to talk, and I've used up the time."

Naturally, they didn't let him go, and that's how Reb Shabsi made his three-minute appeal.

**Reb Yisrael Kalman Poznansky**, the *gevir* of Lodz, happened to be in Frankfurt. While there, he met with Baron Shimon Zev Rothschild, and their conversation ranged over many different topics. When the issue of charity came up, the Baron asked Reb Poznansky what he had done to help the poor of Lodz.

Reb Poznansky answered, "I don't ignore people's needs. I've built hospitals, and I also erected a fence around the cemetery."

The Baron shot back, "That's all well and good for the sick and the dead, but what are you doing for the living?"

**Reb Moshe Wittenberg** was one of the wealthy men of Yerushalayim in the late 1800s. He and Reb Zalman Chaim Rivlin were good friends. Whenever Reb Zalman Chaim would go out to collect charity, he would stop at the Wittenbergs' home for a donation. Once he came to the house and the conversation went as follows:

"Good morning, Moshe."

"Good morning to you, Reb Zalman. What can I do for you?"

"I came to see how you're feeling, Moshe."

"Thank G-d, I feel well. Why do you ask?"

"I heard that you were ill."

"Who could have told you such a thing?"

"Shlomo Hamelech."

"Oh really? How so?"

"Simple. Shlomo Hamelech said, 'There's a bad sickness: the owner guarding his riches.'"

"I didn't know I was so sick, Reb Zalman, but now that you did the mitzva of visiting me, you can leave."

"Not yet, my friend. Anyone who visits the sick takes away a sixtieth of the illness. I still haven't gotten anything from you."

**After all of this talk** about the sharpness of the tzaddikim, one last point needs to be made. Sometimes their naivete or lack of sophistication is their greatest asset. Reb

Fischel of Strykov was a tzaddik who was so immersed in his holy studies that money had no meaning for him. He used to call a gold ruble, which had a reddish tinge, a *roiteh pruta* (a red penny).

When people came to him to give him money to distribute to charity, he would always ask for *roiteh prutas*. When they asked him why he wanted "red pennies," he would answer in all innocence, "Because that's the kind of coin the poor people always accept from me with a smile."

**Reb Nachumke of Horodna** was renowned for his total dedication to deeds of kindness and charity all his life. He went from door to door and store to store, collecting funds for the needy. It made no difference to him who was in need — widows, orphans, *agunos*, or just regular people who were down on their luck. Reb Nachumke felt their suffering and pain, and would help provide for them from one week to the next.

Once Reb Nachumke went in the middle of the night to solicit funds from a wealthy man who had come to town. When Reb Nachumke reached the inn, however, the gates were already locked for the night. What should he do? By morning, the rich man would be long gone!

The wall was too high to climb, so Reb Nachumke decided to dig under it and crawl through to the other side. When his head emerged from the hole he had dug, the night watchman sounded the alarm, since he thought he had found a thief. Everyone came running, only to discover that the supposed thief was none other than the saintly Reb Nachumke! They invited him into the inn, where the rich man gave him a generous donation.

**Reb Nachumke fell ill** at the end of his days and suffered a great deal. Even so, he never stopped going out to collect money for the poor. One night as he made his rounds, he was seized by weakness and sank to the ground. It was late, and no one was around. As Reb Nachumke lay there on the cold, hard earth, a horseman riding by heard his groans. He reigned in his horse and went to investigate the sounds.

The man found Reb Nachumke hovering between life and death. He quickly picked up the elderly tzaddik, put him on the horse, and started to take him home. On the way, Reb Nachumke insisted on being let off.

"But where could you possibly go in the state that you're in? I'm taking you home."

"No," repeated Reb Nachumke. "I still have to collect money for the people who are depending on me."

The man on the horse cried out, "But you're not well, and it's so late."

Reb Nachumke reasoned with him. "Tell me, if you stood to make a big profit by it, would you go into the forest right now?"

The forest at night was a dangerous place, filled with wild animals and bandits, yet the horseman's response came swiftly. "For a large profit, I would certainly go there. I have a wife and five children depending on me."

"Exactly!" cried Reb Nachumke. "You have only six people to care for. What shall I do, when I have hundreds of people relying on me?"

**I once went to a *baal habayis*** for a donation. Now, this *baal habayis* had given me the same one hundred dollars for several years running, but during the last few years he had cut it down to seventy-two dollars. When I asked him why he had cut down his regular contribution, the man told me that his financial circumstances didn't allow him to give what he had in the past. After spending a little time talking with him, I picked myself up to leave.

"Can't you stay and schmooze a while?"

I told him that if he wanted me to, I would come back some other time to have dinner and chat. But on one condition — that I would get another twenty-eight dollars out of him.

The *baal habayis* agreed!

**Another time, I went to solicit funds** from a very wealthy *baal habayis* who lived on the West Coast. I didn't call for an appointment; I just walked in cold.

The *baal habayis* received me very graciously, but nevertheless, when it was time for me to go, he said, "I'm very sorry, Rabbi. I just can't help you."

I went back the next year, and it was the same story all over again.

I went again the third year. You might ask why. Well, as long as a *baal habayis* is gracious, I just keep on trying. All I have to lose is twenty or thirty minutes. So, I went back the third year, and he handed me a check for a thousand dollars.

I asked him why he had given so generously that year when he had given me nothing but the time of day before. He answered, "The first year, I didn't know you, so why should I help you? The second year was pretty much the same story. How well did I know you already? But by now, you're like an old friend. That's why I gave you a check."

**Once, I knocked on a person's door** and asked for Rabbi Katz. The man at the door told me that the rabbi had moved, and that if I'd wait only a moment, he'd get me the new address right away. It turned out that the family had moved only two blocks away, so I decided to head right over to see them.

After Rabbi Katz let me in his home, he told me that he was amazed.

"Just this morning," he said, "I went down to the post office to complain that none of my mail has been forwarded to my new address. Yet, every single fund-raiser that comes to town manages to find my new house right away!"

I said, "I guess when you draw a paycheck, you only do your job. When you work for a Torah institution, though, G-d helps you along so that you manage to go the extra mile, and you can succeed if you really want to. The trick is, you really have to want to."

**Here's a story about someone** who really wanted to succeed. One day, a woman in southern Florida heard loud knocking at her door. She opened it and saw a fund-raiser standing there. The fund-raiser showed her the receipt from their donation of the previous year, and he asked if she could give the same amount again.

The woman apologized and explained that her husband wasn't home, and that she had only one check in the house with which she was going to have to pay for medication for her three sick children when the delivery arrived. The fund-raiser turned away, and she closed the door behind him, assuming that was the end of it.

No sooner had she closed the door, than he was back knocking again.

"How much is the bill?" he asked. "That way, I can give you cash for the medication, and you can just add the amount to the donation."

"I don't know exactly what the bill will come to," she said. "Sorry."

Two minutes later, he was back at her door, asking if she knew when the delivery was supposed to arrive. "Maybe it's worthwhile to wait?"

"Sorry, but I don't know."

After another two minutes, he was knocking at her door

once again. This time, when she opened the door, she saw the fund-raiser standing there with the medication in one hand and the receipt for it in the other. He had already paid for it.

She wrote him a check for the institution, plus the cost of the medicine.

**Even fund-raisers have their limits**, though. After all, we're only human.

Reb Boruch was always raising money for the needy. It made no difference who or what. There was always a need, and Reb Boruch always came through. He raised hundreds of thousands of dollars, and he himself lived like a pauper. He never took a penny for himself.

On one occasion, someone called him up saying that he needed money to buy his children clothing. He named an amount he thought would cover the outlay. Reb Boruch said not to worry, that he would give him the money. The caller then asked if he could also have an additional sum to buy a pair of shoes for one of the children who needed it desperately. Reb Baruch again told him not to worry.

Reb Boruch was very close to Rav Shlomo Zalman Auerbach.

Right after Reb Boruch got married, he kept up doing his work and would come home at very late and fall asleep from sheer exhaustion. Reb Boruch's wife wasn't exactly crazy about this schedule and would have liked him home earlier. One day, she told Rebbetzin Auerbach how bothered she was by her husband's schedule. The rebbetzin mentioned this to Reb Shlomo Zalman, and when Reb Boruch came by the next time, Reb Shlomo Zalman asked Reb Boruch about his schedule. When Reb Boruch told over his schedule, Reb Shlomo Zalman told him that he had to change his schedule and that he should be home by 9:00 p.m. at the latest.

For the next two years, once a week, every week, Reb Shlomo Zalman asked Reb Boruch what time he came home and made sure he was not overdoing it.

**A fund-raiser we'll call** Rabbi Shlomo Leader was on
a fund-raising trip to Europe. He had decided that he would stay
over for Rosh Hashana to complete his mission.

When it came time for Yom Tov, he decided he would be
better off davening in his hotel room instead of going to any of
the shuls in the neighborhood. He was concerned that the local
shuls might not be of the standard he was used to.

After Rosh Hashana, Rabbi Leader remembered that he had
forgotten to say Kaddish for one of his parents and was very
*tzubrochen.* When he came back to Eretz Yisrael, he went straight
to the Chazon Ish and told him what had happened, adding,
"I'm finished as far as fund-raising goes. I don't want something
like this to happen again."

The Chazon Ish told Rabbi Leader that he was mistaken. He
*had* said Kaddish. Every second he was busy raising money for
Torah, was being *yisgadal veyiskadesh Shemei rabba,* and therefore
he should continue what he was doing.

**The fund-raiser of Kollel Chazon Ish,** one of the
biggest *kollelim* in Bnei Brak, woke up one morning with terrible
pains in his feet. He went to a top doctor, who, after a thorough
examination, told him he had multiple sclerosis in his feet, and that
he would have to stay off his feet and rest for the next eight weeks.

The fund-raiser's first thought was to ask if he could continue to travel on behalf of the *kollel.*

"If you go to a hotel, and people come to see you there,
fine," said the doctor. "But under no circumstances can you run
around for your usual fifteen hours a day."

As per the doctor's instructions, the fund-raiser went home
to recuperate. One day, Rabbi Chaim Kanievsky, the son of the
Steipler, came to pay him a visit. Reb Chaim's driver ran upstairs

first to make sure the fund-raiser was home. When he knocked at the door, the fund-raiser told him he couldn't let him in because his wife had gone out, and she had locked the door behind her.

The driver went back to Reb Chaim and told him the door was locked.

"How did you talk to him?" Reb Chaim asked.

"Through the door," answered the driver.

"Good," said Reb Chaim, getting out of the car. "I'll also talk to him through the door."

From outside the locked door, Reb Chaim told the fund-raiser, "The *kollel* needs you. You should have a *refua sheleima.*"

The fund-raiser then managed to hobble to his porch to see Reb Chaim and to say good-bye. Again, Reb Chaim told him to have a *refua sheleima.*

When the fund-raiser turned to go back in the living room, he discovered that, lo and behold, he didn't have any pain. He was so happy, he started dancing around the room.

Right then, his wife walked in and stood stock-still in astonishment.

He told her the whole story.

When he went back to the doctor, he strode into the office like a healthy man. The doctor was very surprised, to say the least. After hearing the story, the doctor examined him again, and told the fund-raiser there wasn't even a hint he had been sick. He did advise him to be careful, though, since the multiple sclerosis could return.

When the fund-raiser heard this, he went back to Reb Chaim and told him what the doctor had said. Reb Chaim told him not to worry. The multiple sclerosis, he said, would never return. Then Reb Chaim told him that he, Reb Chaim, hadn't done anything special. It was a Gemara in *Berachos* that said, "Don't take the blessings of even a simple person lightly."

"It is decreed in heaven how long a person will be sick," Reb Chaim reminded the fund-raiser. "Now was the time to be healed, and I came at just the right moment."

PS: When I later met the fund-raiser, he told me that the punch line was that Reb Chaim told him they would dance together at the upcoming wedding of his son — which is exactly what happened.

**Persistence pays** — even if the fund-raiser is only persistent by accident. A fund-raiser once called a *baal habayis* to try to get him involved in a campaign to help his yeshiva. After the fund-raiser explained his cause, the *baal habayis*, who wasn't *frum*, said that he was very busy and didn't have any time.

Several days later, this same fund-raiser accidentally called the same *baal habayis* once again. His list of calls needing to be made was long, and he didn't realize that he had already called that number.

When the *baal habayis* answered the phone, he said, "Rabbi, you already called me four days ago, and I already turned you down." He sounded irritated.

The fund-raiser was so stunned by his error that he couldn't think of what to reply.

Several seconds of silence passed. Then, before the fund-raiser could answer, the *baal habayis* changed his tone. "You know, Rabbi, I admire your persistence. Call me after Pesach, and I'll see what I can do for you."

**A man I'll call Mr. Kleinfeld** needed to marry off his daughter. Of course, he didn't have any money. (There wouldn't be any story if he had plenty of money.) Anyway, his wife told him that she had seen in yesterday's newspaper that Mr. Shulman, a very wealthy man, was in town. Naturally, he was staying at the fanciest hotel in the city.

"Why not go and ask this Mr. Shulman for the money?" she suggested.

It took some time until he worked up the courage, but Mr. Kleinfeld finally managed to get himself into his best suit and head over to the hotel. His heart was full of doubts. Would Mr. Shulman be in when he got there? Would he be able to get in to see him?

Eventually, Mr. Kleinfeld got to the hotel and made his way up to the imposing entrance. He spotted the doorman, glanced down at his own shoddy suit, and began to worry again. Maybe the doorman wouldn't even let him in!

Looking at the entrance, he told himself, "Kleinfeld, you're here anyway. You might as well try your luck." Oddly enough, though he approached the entrance expecting an argument, the doorman just opened the door and motioned him into the ornate lobby.

Mr. Kleinfeld stopped to plan his next move. Now he had to find this Mr. Shulman somewhere in this huge, fancy hotel. He thought that his best move would be to go over and ask at the desk, but when he realized how unlike the rest of the well-dressed people milling around the lobby he looked, he thought better of it. Maybe they would throw him out!

However, with no other solution in sight, he had no choice. Reluctantly, he made his way over to the reception area, where the clerk on duty asked him what he could do for him. Our friend Kleinfeld didn't know what to say, but since he had no other response prepared, he simply asked for Mr. Shulman. The clerk gave him the room number, no questions asked, and polite-ly said, "Please go right on up."

Mr. Kleinfeld eventually found his way up to the room, but on the way he had ample time to fret. Maybe this Mr. Shulman would be busy, or maybe he wouldn't want to receive guests. Maybe he was in a bad mood. Our poor friend figured, though, that if he'd already come this far, he might as well continue.

Mr. Kleinfeld found the room, knocked gingerly at the door, and immediately found himself face to face with Mr. Shulman. The wealthy man invited the poor man in and offered him a seat.

Kleinfeld was at a loss. How could he get the conversation going? His thoughts ran like this: *I really need twenty thousand dollars for the wedding. But I don't want to come off as seeming greedy.* He started right in and told Mr. Shulman all about his trouble, but instead of asking for the full amount he needed, he asked for ten thousand dollars.

Mr. Shulman calmly pulled out his checkbook and wrote a check for the entire ten thousand dollars. With a hearty handshake and wishes of mazel tov, he wished Mr. Kleinfeld the best of luck, and showed him out the door.

Now, if Mr. Kleinfeld had gone in there prepared to say, "Mr. Shulman, my daughter is getting married. You probably think I'm biased, but she is the best girl around. She will make a fantastic wife and will be the wonderful mother of future generations of Torah scholars and leaders of the Jewish people. What more could you ask for?" Don't you think that would have made a powerful impression? Don't you believe that he would have walked out of there with the entire twenty thousand dollars?

**Rabbi Levi Yitzchak of Berditchev** once went out to raise money for *pidyon shevuyim*. Although he traveled from town to town, he still hadn't come up with the amount he needed.

The thought crossed his mind that he would have been better off staying at home where he could have used his time to study Torah.

In the town he was in, a thief was caught red-handed and thrown into prison.

Reb Levi Yitzchak went to see him, and asked him, "What do you plan to do now?"

The thief said jauntily, "My luck was down today, but tomorrow is another day! I'll be luckier tomorrow."

Reb Levi Yitzchak repeated the thief's words to himself: "Today wasn't too good. But tomorrow will be better!" and he continued on his fund-raising mission.

**Going the extra mile** to raise money for a worthy cause is a Jewish tradition. To construct the famed Yeshivas Chachmei Lublin, its *rosh yeshiva*, Rav Meir Shapiro, traveled the length and breadth of Europe, the United States and Canada to raise the enormous sum needed.

At first, his pleas for financial contributions fell on deaf ears. His vision of a yeshiva for outstanding *bachurim* that would include room and board seemed an impossible dream to many. He ignored the naysayers and continued his efforts to raise funds for the yeshiva. To do so, he was willing to humble himself countless times. In fact, the first one thousand dollars he collected for the yeshiva came because, having no other choice, he hired himself out as a chazan for the High Holy Days. His beautiful voice captivated the New York congregation and its *gabbaim*, and they paid him generously.

**When Rav Elchanan Wasserman** was in Belgium raising money for his yeshiva, he asked one of the prominent members of the community to accompany him to visit the people. The other person said that he didn't think it was becoming for someone of Reb Elchanan's stature to have such embarrassment.

Reb Elchanan replied, "If one is to have embarrassment, he will get it one way or another. Better that he should get it for the sake of Torah."

**While he was out raising money**, Rav Shabsi Yudelevitch was asked by a very wealthy man to prepare his son for his bar mitzva. Reb Shabsi agreed and afterward told the boy that he should put on his tefillin every day. If he didn't, he said, the walls would give testimony against him.

The boy assured him that he would.

Reb Shabsi wasn't convinced. They were sitting in the dining room, so he picked up a very expensive golden soupspoon, part of an heirloom set, and declared to the father, "This spoon will give testimony as to whether the boy puts on his tefillin." Having said that, he put the spoon in his pocket.

Several days later when Reb Shabsi was ready to leave, the father asked for the spoon back.

"I told you the spoon would give testimony," said Reb Shabsi, "and I'll prove it tomorrow in shul."

When people heard about this, they all came to see the sight. How would the spoon give testimony? Would it walk into shul and talk?

Once the shul was packed, Reb Shabsi approached the *bima* and declared, "I told you the spoon would give testimony, and now I will prove it." Looking directly at the boy, he told him to take his tallis and tefillin out of their velvet bag.

When the boy did this, the golden spoon fell out, proof that had the boy put on his tallis and tefillin, he would have found the spoon long before.


**Once, during a stay** in the United States, Rav Elchanan Wasserman came to the house of a donor and found a group of men gambling. They wanted to offer him the profits of their card game, but he refused, saying, "I don't accept that sort of money."

The gamblers pointed out to Rav Elchanan that on a previous occasion he had accepted a donation from a place where there was gambling.

"Could it be?" Rav Elchanan was shocked, and immediately asked a friend for a loan — for his practice was to send donations straight to the yeshiva without delay — and hurried to return the donation he had received.

"I don't accept donations from money gained through gambling," he said.

**Reb Nachumke of Horodna**, on the other hand, did accept such money for *tzedaka*. He would collect even in taverns, where the dregs of society hung around playing cards and gambling. He would say, "Just as they are light-headed, so too are they light-handed. They give generously."

One night, he entered a tavern and saw a group of men gambling. In front of each was a pile of money, and each one was arguing that he had won, and that the money in the pot belonged to him.

Reb Nachumke made his way over to the table, gathered up all the money in his hands and quietly said to them, "My children, you haven't won. I have."

**On another occasion** when Reb Nachumke went to solicit donations from the gamblers, the people there were strangers who didn't know him. They started to make fun of him, and some even went as far as to shove the saintly man.

Reb Nachumke wasn't deterred in the slightest, though, and just kept on asking for their money.

One of the fellows suddenly stood up and slapped Reb Nachumke on the face.

Reb Nachumke put his hand to his cheek and said softly, "That was for me. Now, what can you give for the poor?"

The men were so stunned by his reaction that they begged him for his forgiveness and sent him away with plenty of money.

# Charity Saves from Death

In 1937, when Jews in Europe were running for their lives, the father of Rabbi Saul Chill sought to return to America. Before he left, he went to get *berachos* from the *gedolim*.

When he came to Rav Chaim Ozer Grodzenski in Vilna, the *gadol hador* asked him where he was going. Rabbi Chill's father said he was going back to America. When he was asked how, he replied that he had a passport.

"Then you have no problem," said Rav Chaim Ozer. "The Nazi's will never be able to capture America. They [the Jews in America] give too much charity. As it says in *Mishlei*, 'Charity saves from death.'"

# Charity Saves from Death

**I** stopped in to see one of my regular donors, and he told me this amazing story.

"A few months ago," he began, "before my daughter's wedding, I dreamed that she was in an automobile accident. In the dream, I saw it all happen before my eyes. I also saw her walk away from the crash unharmed.

"When I woke up, I was shaken. I told my daughter that I would drive her to wherever she had to go that day.

"Later that day, my daughter called home to say she had met a friend and they wanted to go shopping. She asked if it would be okay to go in her friend's car. I gave my permission, and they went. By that time, the day was almost over, and my nervousness about the dream was gone.

"Several hours later, I got a call from the police telling me my daughter and her friend had been in a terrible accident. They both walked away from it, but the car was totaled completely. They asked me if I could come out to the scene to pick them up.

"When I arrived, I saw the exact same scene I had seen in my dream! It was the same vehicles, the same view, the same everything. But the main point of my telling you this," he said to me, "is to relate what my daughter told me. She said something strange happened to them while they were shopping. A black man dressed in the garb of a priest had approached them and said he was collecting for charity. He asked if they could help.

"My daughter's friend went through her purse, but all she was able to find was a dime. She gave it to the priest. My daughter checked her wallet. The smallest thing she had was a ten-dollar bill, and she gave that to him. The priest thanked them, and, by way of parting, said, 'You really don't know if you're helping another person or an angel.'"

**Make what you want** of the story, but it is well known that *tzedaka* can save a person from death. The *Midrash Tanchuma* relates such a story in *parashas Haazinu*.

A wealthy and learned man was the proud father of an exceptional daughter who was blessed with every sterling quality. She was modest, bright and beautiful. In short, she was everything a young man could be looking for in a wife.

Her first husband died on their wedding night. Her second husband also died on their wedding night. When she married a third time, and the same tragedy occurred, the young widow made up her mind never to marry again. Who knows how many men she could be responsible for sending to the next world!

Meanwhile, her father had a brother who lived far away. He

was very poor, and had a wife and ten children to support. Every morning, this poor brother would take his eldest son with him and go out to the forest to chop wood. They then sold their wood, and that was how they made their living. One day, the poor brother found no customers, and when he saw that they would have no money to bring home for food, he fainted dead away. The eldest son saw what had happened to his father. His heart went out to him, and he decided that the only thing for him to do was to travel to his wealthy uncle and ask for assistance.

When the young man met his uncle, they each asked after the health of one another's family. After speaking for a while, the nephew spoke up with a bold look in his eye. "Uncle," he said, "I have one thing to ask of you, and I won't take no for an answer. May I ask?"

His uncle said, "Yes."

"Swear to me that you won't deny me what I ask of you!" cried the nephew.

His uncle swore to him that he would be happy to give him anything he wanted.

The nephew took a deep breath and said, "I want to marry your daughter."

His uncle began to cry. He told his nephew what had happened to her first three husbands, yet the nephew insisted that he still wanted to marry her.

"If it's money that you need, I'll give it to you without you marrying her!" the uncle cried.

"That's not my request," said the nephew. "Now remember: you've already sworn to me that you won't deny me whatever I ask."

The uncle saw how determined he was, and so he went to tell his daughter about the words that had passed between them. When his daughter heard the story, she began to cry, begging Hashem to protect her cousin.

A short time later, they celebrated their wedding. While they were standing under the *chuppa*, an elderly gentleman approached the groom and said, "During the wedding feast, you will notice a poor man you have never seen before. When you see him, make sure to get up and bring him over to sit next to you. Give him the best of all the food and drink served." Then the old man, who was really Eliyahu Hanavi in disguise, disappeared.

At the wedding feast, the groom spotted an unfamiliar beggar and immediately did all he could to help him. After the meal, the beggar came over to the groom and said, "I'm a messenger of G-d, and I've come to take you away."

The groom begged him for another year or at least half a year. When he was refused, he asked for thirty days of life. No go.

"Won't you just let me have another week to finish my *sheva berachos*?"

Answered the Angel of Death, "Sorry."

"Can I at least go and say good-bye to my wife?" begged the young man.

"All right," answered the heavenly messenger. "But you should know that your wish is being granted only in the merit of the *tzedaka* that you did with me. Make sure you return straightaway!"

The groom ran to his bride, and found her crying and praying, terrified of what was going to happen to her husband. When he told her that the Angel of Death had come to take him, she said, "Let me go talk to him."

She confronted the beggar confidently. "The Torah says that during the first year of marriage a husband can't go to war. He has to stay home with his wife and make her happy. If you take him now, you'll be turning the Torah of truth into falsehood! If you don't accept my argument, I'm ready to go with you right now to plead my case before G-d."

The angel of death said, "Because of your husband's act of charity, I myself will go and ask G-d." He reappeared in an instant and said, "G-d canceled the decree. Not because of your argument, but because of your husband's act of kindness."

While this was going on, the bride's parents were preparing the grave for their new son-in-law. When they heard that the heavenly decree had been canceled, the entire family gathered to give thanks to G-d.

**The story is related** in *Avos DeRebbe Nasan* (chapter 3) of a pious man who always gave *tzedaka* who was once traveling on a boat when a strong wind began to blow, causing the boat to sink. Rabbi Akiva witnessed the ship going down, and appeared before the *beis din* to testify so that the man's wife could remarry. Before he began speaking, the pious man appeared in the room.

"Are you the one who drowned at sea?" Rabbi Akiva asked the man.

"Yes," he replied.

"Who lifted you out of the sea?"

"The *tzedaka* I gave is what lifted me out of the sea," the man replied.

"How do you know this?" asked Rabbi Akiva.

"When I went down into the depths of the sea," the man said, "I heard a great noise from among the waves. One wave was saying to the other, 'We have to run and lift out of the sea this man who gave *tzedaka* all his life!'"

**The holy Ari, z"l,** was once sitting in a field outside of Tzefas with his students, sharing with them the Torah's mysteries. Right in the middle of his discourse, he interrupted himself and cried, "Hurry! Gather some money together and give it to Reb Yaakov Altriz. He is crying about his poverty, and his voice is reaching the very heavens. G-d is getting angry that no one is helping him and is about to send a plague of locusts to devour all of the crops in the fields around Tzefas. If we hurry with the money, the plague might still be averted!"

The Ari, z"l, took the money that his students had put together and handed it to Reb Yitzchak Hakohen with instructions to run to the poor man's house as fast as his feet would carry him.

When Reb Yitzchak arrived at the Altriz home, he found Reb Yaakov crying.

"Why are you crying?" he asked him.

"My water barrel has broken, and I have no means to fix it," answered Reb Yaakov with tears in his eyes.

Reb Yitzchak immediately handed the money to Reb Yaakov, and the poor man's face lit up.

When Reb Yitzchak returned to the Ari, z"l, his teacher told him that the heavenly decree had been canceled. At that moment, a powerful gust of wind blew in their direction, bearing clouds of locusts. The Ari, z"l, called out, "There is nothing to fear. Everything will be fine."

Just then, the wind changed course and carried all the locusts westward toward the sea, where they all drowned.

**In recent years**, a fund-raiser we'll call Rabbi Gross went to see a *baal habayis* at his office. While Rabbi Gross sat in the waiting room, in walked another fund-raiser. While they were waiting to be seen, the second fund-raiser said to the first, "What's your name?"

When the first fund-raiser said he was Rabbi Gross, the second man asked him if he was related to a certain Rabbi Gross from _____.

"That's my father."

"Though you're his son, and a son knows his father quite

well," said the second fund-raiser, "you don't really know him. Let me introduce you to your father." He went on to tell this story.

"In the early 1950s, the Satmar girls' school was on the verge of collapse. It was desperate for funds, and if they didn't come through shortly, there would be no school.

"The Satmar Rebbe, Rav Yoel Teitelbaum, called me in. I was the driver for Reb Yoel at the time, and he told me about the predicament of the school and asked if I would be willing to go to a certain town for two weeks to raise money. I told the Rebbe I would have to ask my wife first, since we were still in *shana rishona*, our first year of marriage. Only if she said it was okay would I be willing to go.

"The next day, I came back to the Rebbe to tell him my wife agreed that I should go.

"'Are you sure?' the Rebbe asked.

"When I again answered in the affirmative, the Rebbe told me I should go to a certain town for two weeks to raise the funds that were so desperately needed. He also told me to stay at the home of a certain person, but not to eat there.

"The first thing I did was to call a driver to take me around. When I got to town, he took me around to the people. After three days, he told me that we were finished. He had gone through his whole list.

I didn't know what to do. Should I go home because I was finished collecting or should I stay in that city for the remainder of the two weeks?

"I called Rabbi Yosef Ashkenazi, who was the Rebbe's *gabbai*, and told him to ask the Rebbe what I should do, and that I'd call back in half an hour. When I called back, Rabbi Ashkenazi told me that the Rebbe said that I should stay there for the remainder of the time.

"I didn't feel too bad because I had come out of town with two thousand dollars, which, at that time, was a very respectable sum. With plenty of time on my hands, I went into shul, picked up a *sefer*, sat down, and began to learn.

"Shortly afterward, your father came into shul. He saw me and, after giving shalom aleichem, asked me what I was doing in town. I told him the story. I said I had seen everyone, but the Rebbe told me to stay in town anyway. Since I had time, I was sitting there learning.

"Your father said I might be right, but he thought there were plenty more people to see. Just to see who was right, he suggested we go together to try to see a few more people.

"Your father drove to a gas station first. We got out, and your father went over to the owner and said to him, 'Mr. Plony, you've told me that you've always wanted a daughter. Here in this album are all the girls in the school. You're going to adopt one, and I want one dollar a day for the whole year for that girl.'

"Fifteen minutes and $365 later, we were off to the next person, and that's the way it went for the remainder of the time. After two whole weeks, I came out with twenty thousand dollars, which literally saved the school."

End of story? Not yet.

"Several years later," the fund-raiser continued to relate to Rabbi Gross's son, "I went back to this city to raise money, and one of the first stops I made was your father's house. He opened the door and invited me in.

"I immediately noticed a change in him. He was definitely not the same upbeat, positive person who had helped me collect for the girls' school. Something was troubling him, that was obvious.

"It turned out that the rebbetzin, your mother, was ill at that time, hospitalized, in fact. Your father told me her blood count was way down, and her resistance was low. The doctors couldn't figure out what the problem was.

"Your father gave me a check, and I left."

End of story? Not quite.

"After giving me that donation," the fund-raiser said, "your father had a sudden inspiration. He called his wife's doctor and told him that his wife was taking a certain medication to treat an eye problem. Your father told the doctor that he remembered learning in *Eruvin* that this medication, while being good for the eyes, may actually be detrimental to the blood count. He suggested that it might be a good idea to discontinue the eye medication.

"The doctor was very skeptical but, out of respect for your father, said he would look into it and call him back.

"Half an hour later, the doctor called to say that after doing some research into the matter, he found that what your father had told him was true, but only in one in a million cases.

"They decided to give it a try. They discontinued the medication, and the next day your mother's blood count started a slow but steady return to normal.

"Meanwhile, after I left your father's house, I made a beeline for the closest telephone and called Rabbi Ashkenazi. I asked him to tell the present Satmar Rebbe to go to Monroe and pray at the previous Rebbe's grave site for a speedy recovery for your mother, which he did."

End of story? This time, yes.


**Rav Mordechai Gifter** once approached a man in his eighties to ask for a donation of five thousand dollars. The elderly man said, "I don't just give out that kind of money! What do you have to offer in exchange?"

Rav Gifter answered, "I can guarantee you another five years of life."

The man said that he would think it over.

Not long after this unusual exchange, the older man went to see Rav Gifter and asked him if his offer had been genuine.

When Rav Gifter said yes, the elderly man pulled out a contract drawn up by his lawyer. He said, "If you really meant what you said, then please sign on the dotted line, and I'll be glad to give you a check for five thousand dollars."

Rav Gifter signed.

Five years later, the elderly man returned to Rav Gifter and asked if he would like to renew their contract on the same terms.

"I can't sign it again," Rav Gifter said, "but I can guarantee you that the years that you have left will be peaceful."

The elderly man passed away three years later, and his last three years were peaceful ones.

**Reb Yedidia Yechiel Michel Gutfarb** of Jerusalem was a renowned distributor of charity.

One day, a woman approached him saying that she desperately needed a piece of chicken to eat. Rabbi Gutfarb explained that he only had two small chickens in the refrigerator, barely enough for his family for the upcoming Yom Tov. The woman however, pleaded, insisting she was desperate.

Rabbi Gutfarb finally gave in and went to his refrigerator. When he opened the door, he found his three-year-old son inside. The boy's skin had already turned blue.

Thanks to the mitzva of *tzedaka*, the child was saved.

**Binyamin Hatzaddik** was in charge of the charity fund. Since he helped a woman and her seven children survive, G-d added on another 22 years to his life (*Baba Basra* 11a).

The Vilna Gaon explains that a person who gives charity and speaks kindly to the recipient is blessed with 11 blessings. Since Binyamin Hatzaddik acted in such a way toward this woman and her 7 children, he was granted 11 X 8 blessings, for a total of 88 blessings. Since each blessing lasts 3 months (*Sota* 20a), he gained a total of 88 blessings X 3 months, which equals 264 months. Dividing this by 12, the number of months in a year, gives a total of 22 years.

Many people came to the Vilna Gaon for advice or a blessing. He would always ask them for money, not for himself, but rather because giving tzedaka would help them. The Chofetz Chaim says it's not so much the blessing that helps, but the charity.

**Reb Elazar Moshe Horowitz,** the head of the *beis din* of Pinsk, once went out to collect money for the mitzva of *pidyon shevuyim*, redeeming captives. At the time, a very wealthy family known for its *yiras Shamayim* and generosity lived on the outskirts of Vilna. Their home was in the middle of a small forest, and their isolation and wealth made them afraid of all the thieves who roamed the countryside during the nights, vandalizing and robbing the innocent. For this reason, the family bought a pack of watchdogs. During the day, the dogs were tied up, but at night they were let loose to patrol the forest. Because thieves sometimes tried to give poisoned meat to the dogs, the family made a habit of going to bed armed. That way, if an intruder succeeded in reaching the house, they would be able to defend themselves.

Late one night, the family heard the sound of someone knocking on their front door. They wondered how anyone had gotten past all the dogs. Had they all been killed?

They jumped out of their beds, fully armed, to investigate.

"Who's there?"

A voice answered, "It is me, Elazar Moshe Horowitz."

The entire family was at a loss. What had happened to their dogs? Why were they silent? Furthermore, what on earth could the tzaddik, Reb Elazar Moshe, want from them in the middle of the night?

They quickly opened the door to receive the tzaddik and couldn't believe their eyes. The entire pack of dogs was standing right behind Reb Elazar Moshe, and not one was making a sound.

Reb Elazar Moshe apologized for waking them, and quickly explained that though he had been soliciting charity for *pidyon shevuyim* the entire day, he still hadn't collected the entire sum.

"It's essential to collect all the money before dawn, which is why I've come to you so late in the night."

The family gave him enough money to make up the difference, and Reb Elazar Moshe took his leave.

The still-silent pack of ferocious dogs followed him all the way to the edge of the forest.

**On one of Rav Elchanan Wasserman's** fund-raising trips to America on behalf of the yeshiva in Baranovitch, he stopped at the home of a person who had purchased a vicious watchdog. The family had taken that step because the husband was often away on business, and his wife was too scared to stay alone with the children.

When Reb Elchanan arrived at their door, the dog naturally leaped up to the window to see who was coming. As soon as he laid eyes on Reb Elchonon, however, he suddenly seemed to have been struck dumb. The brute didn't so much as whimper all the while Reb Elchonon was in the house, which was nearly an hour.

The moment Reb Elchonon crossed the threshold to leave, the watchdog went back to its stance, ready to attack any intruder.

**Once, a certain *rosh yeshiva*** resolved to raise money for a widow. She needed something to the tune of fifty thousand to sixty thousand dollars, and you can be sure that raising it wasn't easy. This rosh yeshiva — despite the fact that he had an interest in making sure that his "baby" (the yeshiva) was provided for before anything else — expended great effort, and collected the sum for her.

The very next day, while he was at home, the boiler went out. Suspecting nothing, he went down to the basement to relight it. He didn't know that a great deal of gas had escaped, and the basement was full of toxic fumes.

When he struck the match, the gas exploded, rocking the entire building on its foundations. Yet he walked away with nothing worse than a singed beard!

He feels certain that the merit of his help to the widow was what protected him.

**In the Radin Yeshiva,** a *gemach* was run by the *talmidim*. Once, the Chofetz Chaim asked one of the yeshiva's most esteemed *talmidim* to take over the running of the *gemach*. The student, who was an exceptional *masmid*, refused, saying that he wanted only to learn Torah, and therefore didn't have time for the *gemach*.

In response, the Chofetz Chaim opened the Gemara *Rosh Hashana* to page 18a and pointed to the text.

Abaye and Rabba, it says, were both descendants of the house of Eli, whose family members all died young. Because Abaye and Rabba studied Torah, they lived longer. However, Rabba, who studied Torah, lived forty years, while Abaye, who studied Torah *and* did acts of *chessed*, lived sixty years.

**Centuries ago,** a man named Ben Sever was renowned for fulfilling to his utmost the mitzva of giving *tzedaka*.

Once, he heard of an orphan in a nearby country who was engaged but didn't have the money to get married. Ben Sever emptied his home of possessions and gave them to the orphan.

To return home, Ben Sever had to cross a river four *parsa* wide. This river was inhabited by an alligator that attacked anyone who tried to go across. For Ben Sever, though, the alligator turned itself into a bridge and allowed Ben Sever to cross the river on his back.

On the other side of the river, Ben Sever met a very ugly man who asked him if he was Ben Sever and where he was coming from.

When Ben Sever told him all that had happened, the man said, "Your time has come to die."

Ben Sever turned green. Looking heavenward, he said, "Master of the universe, should someone who is constantly immersed in Torah and *chessed* die at a young age? Should I die outside my home like an animal without any other human being around?"

At that moment, a heavenly voice announced, "You have time to go home and get into bed."

Ben Sever departed from the Angel of Death and continued on his way until he came upon a city. When he asked if there was a wise man with whom he could speak, he was told to go see Shefifon ben Laish.

Shefifon listened to Ben Sever's story and told him not to worry. "I'm sure G-d will save you."

Five days after their meeting, a big cloud hovered over the houses in Shefifon's city. When his students mentioned the phenomenon to him, Shefifon told them to go see if the cloud was over the whole city or only over his house. They left, and the Angel of Death came to Shefifon and told him to hand over the deposit with which he had been entrusted.

"To which deposit are you referring?" Shefifon asked.

"Your life," said the Angel of Death. "The time has come to take your life and that of Ben Sever."

Shefifon refused.

When the Angel of Death reported to G-d what Shefifon said, G-d instructed him, "Go back to Shefifon and tell him that you only came to get Ben Sever."

The Angel of Death did so, but Shefifon refused a second time.

Then and there a heavenly voice was heard saying, "What should be done to these two tzaddikim who won't let the decree be fulfilled? Let the decree be nullified and another seventy years added to the life of each."

**How about this** for an unforeseen future benefit of giving *tzedaka*? My friend's yeshiva used to send the boys out on Purim to raise money for the poor in *Eretz Yisrael*. One year, he and a group of friends went to a certain home for a donation on *motzaei Shushan Purim* — not on *Purim*, not on *Shushan Purim*, but the night after *Shushan Purim*. When they walked into the house, they saw the dining room table set for a party, and they couldn't understand why.

The *baal habayis* saw their confusion, so he explained. "Last year was a very hard year for me. Business was terrible, and my marriage was falling apart. When you came to my house for a donation last year on the night after *Shushan Purim*, I was out in the car with my wife, talking about a divorce. When you saw us in the car, you came over and schlepped me into the house and started dancing with me. I was so *tzubrochen* out there in the car, but once you brought me into the house and started singing and dancing, things started to look up. That was the turning point in my business and my marriage, and it was what gave me the strength to weather the storm and hold on until everything came back together.

"Afterward, I decided that I would throw a party for you boys every year on that night. I'll always celebrate on this evening as though it was my anniversary!"

**Many years ago,** Rav Elchanan Wasserman traveled to England to raise funds. Unfortunately, the country was in the middle of a financial crisis when he arrived, so he had a very difficult time of it. He even had a hard time finding someone to drive him around. After repeated attempts, he finally found a man who was willing, despite the fact that the man was far from the yeshiva world.

At the end of Reb Elchonon's visit, this gentleman asked the rabbi for a blessing, and Reb Elchonon blessed him with a complete recovery. This fellow couldn't make out what Reb Elchonon was getting at, but he didn't ask any questions and left it at that.

Several years later, the man suffered a massive heart attack that was followed by a stroke. He slipped into a deep coma, and his doctors declared that there was nothing more to be done for him. They said it was only a matter of time.

While the man lay unconscious, he had a dream that Reb Elchonon came to him and told him not to worry, since he would be having a complete recovery. And, indeed, he did come out of the coma, and he did recover.

After his miraculous recovery, this man was instrumental in raising seven hundred thousand dollars for the Manchester Yeshiva. That is above and beyond all the money he raised for other yeshivos. Whenever he walked into the *beis medrash*, the Manchester Rav would always stop whatever he was doing to go and greet the man personally.

**A friend of mine** once had to go out of town for some reason, but the weather conditions were terrible and visibility was almost nil. My friend's wife prevailed on him to use the car with the four-wheel drive instead of their regular car.

After driving for several miles on a dark, deserted road, my friend went into a bad skid. It was so bad that when his body was finally found several hours later, he appeared to be dead. He was rushed to the hospital, where doctors later told him that he was a very lucky man. His car had been completely demolished, and, they said, he was fortunate to be alive to tell the tale.

After he was released from the hospital, my friend returned to the scene of the accident. After much searching at the site, he was able to retrieve only three items: his tallis, his tefillin — and the little black book where he recorded all his charitable donations and loans to Torah institutions. This, he felt, is what saved him from certain death.

# "C" Is for Collector

Rav Isser Zalman Meltzer was once walking to Etz Chaim Yeshiva to give a *shiur*, accompanied by a *talmid*. On the way, it began to rain, so the two began walking faster. Suddenly, a man stopped them and asked them for *tzedaka*.

As the rain kept pouring down, Rav Isser Zalman searched through his pockets for something to give. After he found a coin and gave it to the man, the two resumed walking.

"It wasn't right for him to make us stand there in the pouring rain, especially when you're in a hurry to say a *shiur*," the *talmid* commented.

Rav Isser Zalman replied, "My job is to give *shiurim*, and his job is to collect *tzedaka*. Who knows which job is more important in *shamayim*?"

# "C" Is for Collector

**W**hether you call the person a fund-raiser, schnorrer, executive director, president or tax collector (raising money to pay the taxes) is irrelevant. The bottom line is that no yeshiva, school or institution can survive without his services. You may have the most outstanding yeshiva, one that is looked up to by people all over the world, but if you do not have someone out there approaching the public and collecting their donations, you will not survive.

By the same token, the average person is anxious to give his *tzedaka* money to a worthwhile cause. Whether he is tithing 10 percent of his profits (*maaser*), or giving 20 percent (*chomesh*), he wants to get the best value for his charity dollar.

The fund-raiser's job is to bridge the gap between donor and institution. It's really a win-win situation.

**When I started in this business,** I was doing more running around than collecting donations. That time of my life, which I like to call my "formative years" in fund-raising, was spent building a solid list of names: including and eliminating, including and eliminating.

A quarter of a century later, I'm still including and eliminating!

As all fund-raisers know, until you compile a list of donors, until you have the names, you can't make any money. Creating the basic list is pure trial and error. For starters, you need at least one person in every city to provide you with some names. This contact tries his best to help you out by giving you good leads, but every once in a while he's sure to make a mistake.

Back in the days when I was still not established, I went to a certain city. I did all right there, but while I was in town I asked the school principal for a few names of potential donors. I assured him that I wouldn't tell anyone who had given them to me.

Since the principal knew me personally, he gave me two names. I went to the see the first one, and I was received so poorly that it just devastated me.

*That's the kind of name he gave me?* I thought in dismay.

At that point, I had no inclination to go and see the second *baal habayis*. But I figured that since he lived right across the street, I might as well. If I had needed to travel as much as three minutes from where I was standing at the time, I would have given up and gone home.

I went into the man's house, and he gave me three hundred dollars. Not only did I get the money from him, I got to know him. The next year I went to him, he raised the amount of his donation.

By the time I stopped going to that city, he was giving me twenty-five hundred dollars every year.

**Once you have a list**, you go to meet the people on it, one by one. A person might be receptive, but then again, he might not. If he's receptive, you might inspire him with your cause. If so, terrific. Then again, he might not care one way or the other.

A fund-raiser never knows just which contact will pan out, so if he's wise, he'll follow them all up. One fund-raiser traveled to a certain town to solicit funds. When he got there, he approached a *baal habayis* and explained his mission. This *baal habayis* then told him to call another *baal habayis* who lived over a thousand miles away in the middle of nowhere. "He's the kind of person who will be interested in your project."

The fund-raiser called up the *baal habayis* who lived off the beaten track, and was invited to the man's home to discuss his project. After two visits, the *baal habayis* wrote out a generous check.

The story doesn't end there, though. Not long afterward, this *baal habayis* became the president of the institution. Some time after he took over the position, the institution called him to say they were unable to cover their payroll. The *baal habayis* told them not to worry. By the next morning, the fund-raiser found a check on his desk to cover the entire shortfall. The salaries were paid on time, but to this day, the fund-raiser has no idea how the check got there.

**Keeping the list up-to-date** is important. Years ago, one of the large car manufacturers came up with an advertising slogan: "America on the move," and it's true. My own experience has been that most people move from city to city, and that when Jews move, they tend to move to a city that is also on the "route," meaning, from one big Jewish town to another. The reasons for this are obvious — they need schools, shuls, a Jewish environment, and all the other necessities of Jewish life. So I usually have no problem tracking down these *baalebatim*, no matter how "on the move" they might be.

One trick of the trade for locating donors who have moved is to ask their relatives, friends or neighbors for the new address. They may give the complete address, or just a street name, or even just the name of the city. Usually, it's not too difficult to find a person once you have the name of the city. One of the best ways to track people down is by calling their old phone number. You'll often get the new number or the new address.

Once, when I was building up my list, I met someone who lived "outside the ghetto," and, over the years, we became good friends. One year I came to see him, only to discover that he and his wife had moved. I couldn't ask the local school for a forwarding address for the simple reason that, though they had been married for many years, they had never had children. I also didn't know where he davened, so that was strike two. I finally found someone who knew to which city he had moved, and, more important, in which neighborhood his parents lived. I tracked them down, called, and they gave me his number.

That year, as always, I went to see him. When I reached his door, I saw a sign that practically screamed, "*Mazel tov*! It's a girl!"

As soon as I saw that, I felt the air go right out of me. It looked as though he had moved again. Rather than give up, I decided I'd ask the new tenants for the forwarding address. I figured that with a sign saying "*mazel tov*," they must be Jewish.

I was buzzed in as soon as I rang the bell, and there was my friend standing at the top of the stairs yelling, "*Mazel tov! Mazel tov*! Your timing is perfect! I just brought my wife and daughter home from the hospital. Thank G-d, everything went all right. My wife is fine, my daughter is fine, and I'm fine!"

This was the highlight of that trip to the States. I was so overjoyed for them, parents at last after waiting so many years.

Seeing them taught me that it is absolutely forbidden to ever give up hope. It doesn't matter what anyone says, no matter who or what kind of an expert they are supposed to be. In my friend's case, there were doctors claiming it would never happen, but why believe them? There is a higher court than the highest court in the world, and that is G–d's will.

You're probably thinking that this couple was married for ten or fifteen years before they had their daughter. Wrong. They had been married for twenty-one years. Never give up hope.

**People wonder if the goal** of fund-raising, which is raising money, couldn't be accomplished with less running around. One fund-raiser, after a long and exhausting trip collecting money for a yeshiva, asked this question of Rav Chaim of Volozhin.

"Why is it," he said, "that when a university needs money, one of their fund-raisers goes out and brings back big money right away, but when a fund-raiser for a yeshiva goes out, he has to drag himself halfway around the world? Even then," he continued, "after he's all worn out from traveling and knocking on doors, he comes away with only enough money to see the yeshiva through for a short while."

"This is pure *hashgacha*," Reb Chaim answered. "Since the universities teach *apikorsus*, it's better that their fund-raisers get their money and leave town quickly, before they spread their heresy any further.

"We, on the other hand, are trying to strengthen Torah. Our fund-raisers invariably spread Torah wherever they go, by speaking in shuls or telling their *vertlach* here and there. In that sense, the more time they spend on the road, the better off the Jewish people are!"

**Rav Moshe Aharon Stern**, who used to travel all over the world to raise money for his institution, is a prime example of a fund-raiser who had a big impact on people wherever he went. Once, a fellow he didn't recognize approached him on the street in Eretz Yisrael saying, "Shalom aleichem. Do you by any chance remember me?" The man went on without waiting for an answer. "You were in England, weren't you? Didn't you once give a speech at Jack Levinson's house on Tisha B'Av for the people of Stamford Hill?" Jack Levinson was a man who could have twenty or thirty fund-raisers staying at his home at any given time.

"I heard you speak in English," the man continued, "and I was drawn to what you were saying. My wife was not Jewish, which meant that my children weren't either. I had plenty of money. I owned a few supermarkets that were open seven days a week. Yet I was so inspired by your talk that I became a *baal teshuva*. My wife and children converted, I sold my business, and we made aliya. My children all learn in yeshivos now, and it was all because of that talk you gave."

**Even without traveling**, a fund-raiser can have an impact. One *rosh yeshiva* in a major U.S. city tried on many occasions to get a donation from a very wealthy businessman who owned a chain of carpet stores. Not only did he never meet with success, he couldn't even get to see the man. It had almost become a joke, one the whole yeshiva was in on.

One day, out of the blue, the store owner walked into the *beis medrash*. The *talmidim* were in a state of shock, especially when he asked to see the *rosh yeshiva*.

When the businessman entered the *rosh yeshiva's* office, the *rosh yeshiva* could hardly believe his eyes.

The businessman got straight to the point. "Last night, I had a dream. I don't remember all the details, but the message was that if I don't mend my ways, my time in this world is up. I've asked several people what the dream means, and no one can interpret it for me." He paused and then said, "The only common denominator in what they said was that I should ask a rabbi for an explanation, which is why I'm here now."

The *rosh yeshiva* told him the dream meant exactly that, straighten out or else. Then the *rosh yeshiva* said to him, "There are a lot of people who have to straighten out, but it takes special merit to get a warning like this. The question is, why did you of all people have this dream? Did you do anything special in your life?"

"Nope," came the businessman's reply. "Nothing I can think of."

"In that case," mused the *rosh yeshiva*, "perhaps you have *yichus*. Do you have any illustrious ancestors in whose merit you might have had such a dream?"

"I really don't know much about my family tree," said the businessman, "but I've got a cousin who knows the whole family lineage."

On the spot, the *rosh yeshiva* called the cousin. He found out that the person sitting in front of him was a direct descendant of Rav Simcha Bunim of Peshischa.

Not only did this person give him a donation right then and there, but he also became a staunch supporter of the yeshiva. To top it all off, he also started to keep a learning *seder* in the yeshiva.

**Interestingly enough**, many people who are otherwise disconnected from Torah observance give generously. There was a member of the Knesset from the Likud faction who once explained to an observant man his respectful attitude toward the religious community.

"We know that there is the concept of a Shabbos goy. In my home, I try to instill in my children the concept of a Shabbos Jew. I want my children to remain Jewish. I don't want them to intermarry. They therefore need something to look up to.

"Personally, I don't keep Shabbos," he said. "I'm too lazy, I guess, and I don't know enough. But I still want someone to keep Shabbos going. I hope that the fact that there are still Jews keeping Shabbos will help ensure that my children stay within the faith. As far as I'm concerned, religious Jews provide a service for the rest of us, and part of my commitment as a Jew has to do with realizing that they're doing me a service."

**This is why a lot** of nonobservant Jews will support religious causes. By doing so, they try to maintain their connection with Judaism and support Jewish continuity. For this reason, many people are happy to see a religious fund-raiser making the rounds in their neighborhood.

For instance, in one small community in the States, many of the modern and secular Jews wanted to establish a central fund to keep fund-raisers from going around knocking on doors. A man who was very far from *frumkeit* and probably didn't even know how to daven, got wind of the proposal, and announced that he was dead set against it. When asked why, he answered, "If these guys with the beards and *peyos* stop knocking on my door, how will my children have any kind of a connection with the genuine article? I want my children to know that a beard and *peyos* are part of my heritage. My grandfather and great-grandfather looked like that. I may not live that way, but I want my children to know about that kind of Jew, too. The fund-raisers are my connection. And who knows? Maybe some day my grandchildren will wind up in that institution."

**The personal integrity** of a fund-raiser makes an impression. Rav Aharon Kotler once paid a visit to a wealthy person to request a donation for a certain Torah institution. The wealthy man said, "I don't believe in the cause, but since you have come, I will give you something for your yeshiva," meaning, Lakewood Yeshiva. At the time, Rav Aharon was already recognized as the *gadol hador*.

Rav Aharon refused the donation, saying, "I came to you

for a specific purpose, not for my yeshiva."

The donor was so impressed by Rav Kotler's integrity that he went on to become a staunch supporter of both the institution Rav Aharon had come to fund-raise for as well as Lakewood Yeshiva.

**A family was asked** to host several students for the Friday night meal. Since the students were attending a yeshiva for *baalei teshuva*, the host asked where they were from and what made them become religious.

One of the students related that between his junior and senior years of high school, he and his parents decided he would go on a tour of the Holy Land. However, instead of getting the spiritual uplift he expected, he saw only beaches and other secular tourist attractions. In the middle of the tour, he decided he had had enough, and called his parents to ask permission to leave the tour and return home. His parents concurred with his assessment and told him to come home.

The next step was to call El Al to see if he could change his ticket. They told him it would be no problem. After spending all his money on presents, keeping just enough change for transportation, he finally arrived at the airport. When he approached the airline counter, they told him there was a fifty dollar charge to change the ticket.

He explained that he had used up all his money, and that he didn't have a penny left. After arguing for a while and getting nowhere, he finally retreated to a bench, sat down and started to cry.

Among the dozens and dozens of people that passed him, a fund-raiser I know (whose attire identified him as an Orthodox Jew), stopped and asked, in Hebrew, why he was crying.

The teenager said he didn't understand, so the person asked again in Yiddish. Again, the youth said he didn't understand, so the person asked again in English.

Now that they were communicating, the teenager explained his dilemma, that he didn't have the fifty dollars needed to change his ticket. The man took out one hundred dollars and told the youth, "Keep the change for carfare from the airport in the States."

When the boy asked for the man's address so that he could pay back the loan, the man said, "Accept it as a gift. Otherwise, if you take it as a loan and don't pay it back, you'll be guilty of theft."

"Okay," said the youth. "I'll take it as a present, but I'll make sure to have my parents send it back to you."

The man was wrote down his name and address and was in the process of handing it over, when the youth said, "Don't worry. My parents will pay it back with interest."

The man grabbed back the piece of paper and said that that, too, was against the Torah, since a person is not allowed to lend at interest.

Only after the boy said he'd accept the money as a gift and pay it back with no interest did he get the address.

On the long plane trip back to the States, the boy kept thinking about what had taken place at the airport. When he finally arrived home, he told his parents what had occurred and said, "If this is how a religious person acts, then I want to be religious, too. Let me go to a yeshiva."

"After you finish high school and college," his parents said.

"Then how about during summer break?" he asked.

His parents agreed, figuring that by the time next summer rolled around, he would have forgotten the whole thing.

To their surprise, their son did not forget, and has just completed his second year in yeshiva — all thanks to a fellow Jew's kindness.

**Fund-raisers have an impact** on everyone they meet, Jewish or not. Rav Moshe Aharon Stern was once being driven on one of the turnpikes in the United States when his driver was pulled over by a state trooper.

"You're speeding," said the state trooper.

"Aren't there any exceptions to the rule?" the driver asked.

"The only exception is for emergency vehicles like police cars, ambulances and so on."

"To tell you the truth," said the driver, "I feel like I'm in the same category, because I'm taking a rabbi to a very important meeting."

The state trooper looked into the back of the car, took one look at Rav Stern, and said to the driver, "You're right. Follow me."

The state trooper got into his car, turned on his lights and siren, and sped down the highway. The car carrying Rav Stern followed until some twenty-five miles later, when it reached its turnoff.

At the exit, the state trooper waved good-bye.


**The average person** can also have an impact. A fund-raiser once flew on a certain airline, and when he reached his destination, he found that the airline had lost his baggage. While filling out the forms of his claim, he was asked by the airline representative the standard questions.

When he was asked for a phone number where he could be reached, the fund-raiser gave phone numbers in half a dozen cities. "If you can't reach me in one city," the fund-raiser said, "try the next. I'm always on the move."

The airline representative called two days later and said that he had good news and bad news.

"The good news is that we found your suitcase," he said. "The bad news is that it's empty."

"That's okay," answered the fund-raiser. "There was never anything in it. I'm an Orthodox Jew, and I gave my word that I would return the suitcase. I just wanted to keep my word."

**I once walked into** the home of one of our donors, and he told me that he had just returned from the Far East from one of his quarterly business trips. On one occasion, he was doing business with an Asian man when, completely out of the blue, the man asked him if he was an Orthodox Jew.

"Yes, I am," he said, "but why do you ask?"

"I once did business with a man who dealt with me very honestly," he answered. "He, like you, refused to do business with me or anyone else on the Sabbath, even if it meant the loss of large sums of money. During one of our conversations, this man told me he was an Orthodox Jew."

He continued, "Aside from him, I've never seen another Jew in my life, but I noticed that you act the very same way that my old business contact did. I just had to ask if you were Jewish. And I have to say that your honesty and integrity make it a pleasure to do business with people like you."

**Once, I tried to meet** with a certain *baal habayis*, but it seemed that every time I came to his home, he was either busy or at the office. After several fruitless attempts on my part, his wife said to me, "I'm so sorry you have to keep coming back. Let me write you a check now so that you won't have to come again later.

"The truth is," she went on, "the only time I get to see him is on Shabbos. I have a non-Jewish neighbor who is actually very jealous of me! Every Sunday morning, the neighbors go to church. Afterward, they come home, eat together, and then the husband goes out to mow the lawn. Later, they go shopping. What with the phone always ringing, and all of the other things they do on their supposed day of rest, the family never really gets a chance to relax.

"They see how different it is with us. On Shabbos, we all go to shul together, we come home and eat our meal, we relax, take a nap, whatever. That's why my neighbor is so jealous."

Of course, the non-Jewish neighbors can get only a superficial view of Shabbos, without the spiritual richness we enjoy. Yet even on this simple level, our Torah way of life makes a strongly positive impression.

**People can make a *kiddush Hashem*,** or the opposite. A friend of mine once went to someone's house to get a donation. After knocking for several minutes, he realized that the *baal habayis* was just not going to let him in. The doorbell worked and the lights were on, which meant someone was home, but no one was answering the door. What convinced my friend of the futility of his efforts was the face he saw looking out of a second-story window to see who was at the door. Seeing that he wasn't going to get anywhere, my friend finally decided to hit the road and try his luck elsewhere.

Just as he was about to get into his car, an obviously non-Jewish neighbor approached him and said, "While I was washing my car, I saw you knocking. I noticed that someone in the house looked out to see who it was. You're clearly here for a donation, and I don't want you to walk away empty-handed. Please take this hundred dollars."

When the *baal habayis* at the window saw the exchange, he felt so bad that he ran down to give my friend a donation.

**No matter how good the list is,** a fund-raiser is always working to update and improve his clientele. He has to. What if a person's business fails — or worse, G-d forbid? If he's always adding to his list, his institution always has someone else to go to if the situation demands it. This is the part of the business no one sees or appreciates.

Expanding the list is what took me to one quaint town off my usual route, where I met a few interesting people. One of the new donors was a Mr. Smith, a name I found unusual.

"Where does the name Smith come from?" I asked him.

"My parents came from Russia," he told me. "Back there,

Jews didn't have family names. Then one day the government went around taking a census. For convenience's sake, many people took on the name of their profession. My father was a blacksmith, so he called himself 'Mr. Blacksmith.' Later, when my parents came through Ellis Island to be processed for entry into the United States, the official there told them he didn't like the name 'Blacksmith,' because it was too long.

"He took a quarter from his pocket and said he was going to flip a coin to choose a name for them. Heads, and the name would be Black; tails, and the name would be Smith. That's how my father got the name Smith."

It was a fascinating story, but I wasn't finished.

"One more question, if you don't mind," I said. "To what do you attribute your longevity?" He was in his early nineties.

"All my life," he said, "I gave my parents great respect."

Over the years, I've asked a lot of people what merit they had to reach the age of ninety, and they all told me the same thing. They always gave their parents respect.

**Speaking of honoring parents**, a fund-raiser once went to see someone's son for a donation, since the previous year the father had passed away.

"I'll tell you quite frankly," said the son, "I don't have an interest in the same yeshivos that my father did."

When the fund-raiser said that he was hoping the son would continue to give anyway, since his father was on the annual list, the son said, "Then take him off."

The fund-raiser hesitated, and then replied, "I just don't have the heart to cross him off the list. You do it." He handed the list to the son along with a pencil.

The son held the list in his hand and said nothing. After several long moments, he said, "I can't do it."

From then on, he continued to support, in his father's name, the same yeshiva his father had given to for so many years.

**The Chofetz Chaim** strongly approved of such behavior, as seen in this short excerpt from his book, *Ahavas Chessed* (chapter 3):

There are people who, out of love for their deceased parents, want to make some eternal memorial of them, and so have made for them a tombstone of expensive marble, with elaborately carved letters, flowers and designs. They then decorate the gravesite with ornate landscaping, all of which costs a lot of money, and with this the children feel that they are bringing joy to their parents' souls.

How great is their error! After the soul leaves this world, it realizes that in the next world only Torah and mitzvos have any value. A headstone, our Sages say in Tractate *Shekalim*, is important, but it would be better for the children to buy a simple headstone and use the remaining money to buy a set of the Talmud for a *beis medrash* and write inside that it is dedicated in their parents' honor. Alternatively, one could use the money to open a free-loan fund in honor of one's parents. Then, every time a loan was given, or the set of the Talmud was used, the parents' souls would become more elevated.

The holy Shelah writes that when a child does a mitzva, it atones for the sins of his deceased parent and actually has the power to take a parent's soul out of Gehinnom and bring it into Gan Eden to sit among the righteous.

The *Zohar* states that the mitzva to honor one's parents is even more binding after they have died, because a parent's status in the next world depends greatly on the way his children behave in this world.

**Yeshiva fund-raisers** try to live up to their role as ambassadors of the Torah world. For many people, their contact with the fund-raiser may be their only chance to ask questions and get answers.

I once went to see one of my regular donors, a store owner in New York City. This time, he told me he didn't have any money for me.

"You'll have to speak to my son," he said, "and he isn't here now." I was about to leave, when he added, "But why should you lose out? Go across the street to Goldschmidt Shoes and ask for Mr. Goldschmidt. He was once the president of the local (non-Orthodox) shul. Maybe he'll give you something."

I went across the street. When I entered the store and asked for Mr. Goldschmidt, a big, heavyset guy came over to me. I again asked for Mr. Goldschmidt, and he said that was him. I gave him a shalom aleichem.

"What can I do for you?" he asked me.

"I'm looking for a Jewish heart."

"I've got a Jewish heart," he said.

"We'll soon find out," I replied.

We started schmoozing about various things, and half an hour later, he wrote me a check for eighteen dollars for the yeshiva.

Six months later, I had to run into New York. My wife needed a pair of shoes, and, since I saw we wouldn't have time to go elsewhere, I asked her if she wouldn't mind going into this store.

"He seemed to have good merchandise," I told her, "and who knows? We may even get a discount."

We entered the store, my wife found a pair of shoes to her liking, and we got the discount. All the while, we were schmoozing. Mr. Goldschmidt told me his hero was King David. He thought King David was just the greatest.

I told him we had a fantastic book at home about King David, and that he would love it. I told him I did a lot of traveling and said that the next time I was in the neighborhood, I would try to remember to bring him the book.

As things went, I forgot about it. Several months passed, and when I came back to get my annual contribution, he reminded me.

I apologized and told him I would bring it in.

In the meantime, he gave me another donation, and this time he upped it.

A few days went by, and I had the chance to drop off the book. When I went back to get the book, we became immersed in a very long conversation about King David, Judaism and all the things that go with that sort of conversation. We talked for three hours.

Following that discussion, I started giving him other books, such as *The Midrash Says*, which he read from cover to cover. Eventually he finished the whole five books of the Torah.

One day he said he wanted to ask me a question.

"Go right ahead," I said.

"I can't understand the story of the golden calf. After all, the Jews saw the ten plagues in Egypt, the splitting of the Red Sea, the giving of the Torah on Mount Sinai, just to mention a few miracles, and there they go and make a golden calf. How is that possible?"

I told him the various classic answers to this question. But no matter how I tried to explain it to him, no matter what I said, he wasn't happy.

Finally, I said, "You know something? This reminds me of the story you told me about what happened to you in college."

He had told me an unbelievable story. After the graduation ceremony, he and his friends had gone out to celebrate. Well past midnight, he climbed into his sports car, pushed the gas pedal to the floor and hit eighty miles an hour. He lost control of the car, and it flipped over. The next thing he remembered was waking up in the hospital. When he came home from the hospital, he was completely okay. The only reason they kept him in the hospital was for observation. He had no broken bones, not even a scratch. When he saw the car, he couldn't believe he had walked out in one piece with no broken limbs. The car was a complete wreck.

While looking at the car, he said, "G–d, for all intents and purposes, I should be dead. For some reason, You saved me. If the opportunity ever presents itself, I hope that I will be able to answer positively and fulfill the purpose You saved me for."

Now I asked him, "Do you realize that a tremendous miracle happened to you? Your personal miracle was no different from the splitting of the sea. One minute you're driving, and the next, you're in the hospital. You saw the car. You saw this fantastic miracle. You even said so yourself. So what happened to you? G–d made a tremendous miracle for you. Have you changed? Are you a *shomer Shabbos*? Do you put on tefillin every day?"

"Take it easy," he said.

"No, I won't take it easy."

"Listen," he said, "I don't think G–d saved me to put on tefillin every day."

"How do you know?" I asked him. "After all, it's one of the 613 mitzvos. Maybe that *is* why He saved you."

He promised to put on tefillin the next day.

The next day, I called him up to find out if he had followed through on his promise.

"Yes," he said, "I put on tefillin today, but I won't be able to tomorrow."

"Why not?" I asked.

"Because tomorrow, I've got to take my wife's two Doberman pinschers down to the vet, and I won't be able to get to minyan."

"Then daven at home."

"No, you can't daven at home," he said to me. "You've got to daven with a minyan."

"Don't be so *frum*," I told him. "If you can't daven at shul, at least daven at home."

"It's not the same thing," he protested.

"You're reneging on your deal."

"Okay, okay," he said. "I'll put on tallis and tefillin and daven at home."

This was on Thursday. On Friday, I got a frantic phone call from my wife. Mr. Goldschmidt was trying to get a hold of me. I called him, and he told me this story.

"I woke up late, but I promised you I would daven, so I not only said Shema, like you said, but I davened everything. I was running really late, so I skipped breakfast. I took my attache case and the two Doberman's out to the Corvette. I put the case on the roof and somehow managed to shove the two dogs into the car, got in and zoomed off. There I was, weaving in and out of traffic, with everyone beeping me. I felt like I couldn't care less. I had to get to work.

"When I got down to the kennel, the vet told me that my wife called and said not to worry, that she had the attache case and it was only dented.

"'*Oy vey*,' I yelled. I had forgotten the case on the roof of the car. I called my wife to see how she had gotten it. She told me that some guy saw me driving with the case on the roof. 'He tried to beep you,' she said, 'but you kept on going. The case flew off, and he stopped to retrieve it. He opened it, saw your phone number in it and called the house. He even came over to deliver it.' Then my wife said, 'I gave him a $25 reward.'

"Rabbi," he told me, "I had twelve hundred dollars in checks, six hundred dollars in cash and three credit cards inside. *Nothing was missing.*

"I promise that from now on, I'll always put on tefillin."

# "D" Is for Donor

I once stopped at someone's house to get a donation. It was to be my first time meeting this particular *baal habayis*, so I tried to prepare myself mentally with a good opening line. What happened, though, was totally unexpected.

The man of the house came to the door when I knocked and said, "I'm so sorry, but I can only give you a dollar. You're the fifth person who's been here today, and my *tzedaka* account is completely exhausted."

As I was writing out the receipt, he asked in afterthought, "What yeshiva do you represent? Who is the *rosh yeshiva*?"

When I told him, he asked me to wait a minute. He returned with another dollar bill and said, "Like I said, my account has been tapped dry. But at least now I've upped my donation by 100 percent!"

# "D" Is for Donor

**M**aking the rounds, you'll run into some folks who just don't want to know from you, but more often than not, you'll run into a lot of fine people. These are the folks who make a fund-raiser's job a pleasure. I remember one *baal habayis* in particular. I walked into his house for the first time way back in 1970 when I first started raising funds for the yeshiva. I had walked into this man's house on a specific date, which, for practicality's sake, we'll say was April 20. He said he couldn't give me anything that year.

"Okay," I told him. "Have a good year anyway."

"Aren't you going to ask me why?"

To humor him, I asked him why.

"I like to give to institutions only once a year," he said. "Since you came to me on April 21 last year, the full year is not up yet. You still have one more day before you can come back."

He was joking, but I didn't realize it at the time, since I was still new in the field.

He then took out a five-page, single-spaced typed list and showed me that I was just one more name to add.

"And let me tell you this," he added. "I have solid proof that there's no life on the moon."

This was at a time when Russia had already sent up Sputnik, and America was entering the space age.

"What kind of proof?" I asked naively.

Keeping a straight face, he said, "If there was life on the moon, the Ponovezher Rav would have been up there collecting money." Then he gave me the donation.

To my sorrow and that of many, this *baal habayis* passed away a few years later. I was told that any person or yeshiva with a financial problem had always found his door open. People say that at least on one occasion when he was in financial difficulties himself, he went and borrowed money so that all the teachers in the local yeshiva could be paid on time.

**Sometimes the biggest givers** are not the wealthiest. Once I drove for hours on the turnpike to get from one city to another. After all that time on the road, I felt exhausted and grimy. I had just pulled into the driveway of a certain *baal habayis*, when the man came out and shouted, "You should know that you've got a lot of chutzpa!"

Naturally, I was somewhat taken aback. What had I done to deserve that kind of abuse?

Before answering his charge, I put the car into park, turned off the engine, took the key out of the ignition, and turned to face my accuser.

"Okay. What did I do this time?" I asked calmly.

"It's not what you did, but what you *didn't* do."

"Okay," I replied. "What exactly is it that I didn't do?"

"Last year when you came," he answered, "you managed to see every single *baal habayis* in town — everyone, that is, except the *bnei Torah*. They felt that, even though they don't have any money, it was still a chutzpa on your part to deny them some participation in the mitzva."

Needless to say, from then on, every year I went to that community, I would make it my business to solicit funds from the *bnei Torah*.

**Incidentally, I've been warned** on many occasions that *bnei Torah* do not have money, and that I shouldn't bother them. Ironically, I find that, proportional to their income, *bnei Torah* give more than *baalebatim* — and that the *bnei Torah* who don't have any money give the most.

For instance, on a recent trip to the States, I looked up an old friend of mine with whom I had learned in yeshiva years ago. The guy was barely making a living, and I knew that if I went to his apartment, he would be able to give me only a few dollars. Even so, I felt it was worthwhile, because I knew how much he looked forward to my annual visit. He, like many others, still felt a closeness with the yeshiva and appreciated a schmooze with one of the boys from the old days. Visits like that are what keep up that old bond for plenty of guys. So, as unofficial goodwill ambassador of the institution, I tend to consider such visits obligatory, not optional.

The truth is that visiting him amounted to a sacrifice of my time, since there was no way it could be done in ten minutes or less. I knew in advance that I would be with him for about an hour.

That's how I found myself one day sitting in the basement office of the home he had just moved to, doing what comes naturally: reminiscing about the old days. In the course of conversation, I wished him a mazel tov on his new home. He told me he had had no choice but to move. Thank G-d, their family had grown, and their old place just couldn't hold them anymore. He confessed that things were very hard right then, because the monthly mortgage was six hundred dollars over and above what they used to pay.

"Aside from that," my friend continued, "my car has just gone to that great junkyard in the sky. Fortunately, I got my money's worth out of it before it went. It was good up until the very end. When it finally did go, it went out with a real bang. I was driving along one day when it gave a hiss, started rattling and steam burst out of the radiator."

My friend told me he had just paid more than one hundred dollars for a bicycle so he could get to work each day. On top of that, one of his kids needed braces, and another had just gotten stitches that still weren't paid for.

He summed up this brief rundown on his current situation by saying, "Thank G-d, I'm a happy-go-lucky kind of guy. Everything Hashem does is for the best, so why not just make the best of it?"

I wished him the best of luck, and told him to just hang in there.

"I'll be back next year," I said, "and I'll get a check from you then, when you're in a better position."

But he wouldn't hear of it. He insisted on giving me a donation right then and there.

I argued with him. "You know it won't make much of a difference to the yeshiva."

He insisted, though. "We've had days when the kids couldn't get to school because there was no bus fare in the house. But I won't let you out of my house without my check.

I'm going to postdate it for a few months' time, but I want to give it for the sake of the mitzva, and to show my appreciation for all the yeshiva did for me."

I was left with a real problem. He wouldn't let me out of his house without taking his check. Do I take it and tear it up later? It would only upset him. I know he keeps a ledger with a record of every check that doesn't clear his account. My experience has taught me that people who have less tend to give proportionately more money to tzedaka. There's a lot of food for thought in that.

**I once went to the home** of a *baal habayis* and explained why I was there. This happened over twenty years ago. The man was in the rabbinate and had a large family, so he gave me a check for five dollars. This went on for a number of years. At a certain point, he raised me to ten dollars, and that also went on for a couple of years. One year, he handed me a check for eighteen dollars.

When the next year rolled around, I said, "You gave me eighteen dollars last year. Why don't we round it off to twenty-five this year?"

He gave it to me.

By the following year, I was feeling pretty brave so I asked him for twenty-six dollars. "It equals the *gematria* of G-d's Name, you know."

The next year, I asked for "power" (the *gematria* of *koach* is twenty-eight). He said to me, "What will you ask for next year?"

I answered, "Take heart! That will come to thirty-two (*lev*, heart). The year after next will be, of course, thirty-six" (two times *chai*, life).

I was on a roll, but the *baal habayis* interrupted me. "Stop right there. Enough *gematrias*. I'm writing out a check for fifty dollars, and that is going to be my absolute limit."

We took our leave of one another on very good terms, and I still see him every year I travel to the States.

**After seeing a certain** *baal habayis* for many years, one Shabbos in shul he told me to come to him on a certain day. I was curious as to why, since I had heard from several fund-raisers that he had asked them to do the same.

He explained to me that he didn't mind giving *tzedaka*, but actually looked forward to it.

"The only problem is," he said, "if I want to have anything to give, I have to work. Since I put in a lot of hours, I'm often not home. What happens is that since there's no way fund-raisers can know whether or not I'm home, they're constantly knocking on the door. It's reached a point where my wife can't sit down to a cup of coffee or give the kids supper and a bath without the bell ringing.

"Many evenings, the bell does not stop ringing. Whether she wanted to or not, she was forced to answer the door to stop the ringing. If she sends one of the kids to answer the door, the fund-raiser invariably asks, 'Is your father home?' If the kid says his father isn't home, they ask to see the mother.

"When my wife finally found a second to come to the door," he continued, "the fund-raiser would ask when she expected me home and would not let up until she gave him a specific time."

I nodded my head in understanding.

The man went on. "It was starting to get out of hand. Instead of closing the door on giving *tzedaka*, I decided to set a certain amount of time aside each week to issue checks for charity."

I told him I understood.

He kept this up for a while, but every so often a fund-raiser would not have the time to get to him during the scheduled hours. To me, it really never made a difference, because if that *baal habayis* was unavailable when I had the time, the next time I saw him, I would tell him that I missed him on the appointed hour. He would then tell me not to worry, but to come to his office, and he'd issue me a check on the spot.

**There are people** who believe *tzedaka* should be given no matter how good or bad the institution or its representative is. A fund-raiser was once invited to spend Shabbos in the home of a local businessman. During the course of one of the Shabbos meals, the talk at the table turned to a prominent Rebbe. The fund-raiser started to degrade the Rebbe and went off on a tangent about how bad this particular Rebbe was. The *baal habayis* asked him to stop, but to no avail.

The meal ended, and that was it for the time being.

At the end of Shabbos, the businessman took the fund-raiser's suitcase and relocated it to the bottom of the stairs, outside the front door. He told the fund-raiser that he was sorry, but he was no longer welcome in their home, and that if his institution wanted another donation, they should send someone else.

"Since it was Shabbos when you spoke *lashon hara*," the businessman said, "and I did not want you to be without a place to stay, I held myself back from throwing you out right then and there." After a pause, he said, "But this does not take away my mitzva of *tzedaka*," and went on to give the fund-raiser a five-dollar bill. With a "*Gut voch,*" he closed the door and went back inside.

**I once knocked** on a man's door, and when he let me in, I said that I was raising funds for my yeshiva.

The man countered, "The local yeshivos are also suffering. Who will support the local institutions if all the locals are supporting out-of-town yeshivos?" Then he decided to get personal. "Better yet, allow me to rephrase my question. Do you contribute to our yeshivos?"

He may have rephrased his question to put me on the

defensive, but he had definitely started up with the wrong guy. I told him the facts.

"You know, every time that I come into town, I go to visit the local *rosh yeshiva*. He gives me a check for my institution, and I give him a check for his. In other words, we swap checks."

I do this because every fund-raiser still has an obligation to give *maaser*, and because even if no one in the community will know about it, there is still something called expressing one's gratitude toward the community as a whole.

I know of a man who, when he was raising money for himself, heard that the local yeshiva of the town he was visiting was in desperate straits. He felt so bad for the failing institution that he took one thousand dollars of the money he had raised for himself and gave it to the yeshiva.

I've encountered this same attitude among donors, too. Someone once took me to a *baal habayis* to get a donation. After the person seated us at the dining room table, he told us that he gives a donation to everyone who comes to his house. Then he went on to say that no matter what size his donation is, a large or small sum, he writes out a matching check for local institutions. "They are struggling," he explained. "This way, everyone comes out winning."

**People realize that giving** to *tzedaka* brings blessing to the home. One *baal habayis* told me that for the first eight years of his marriage, his finances were a mess. No matter how he set up his budget, it somehow always wound up being way off, leaving him without any money to get him through the month. Even though he gave to charity, he felt he was doing it all wrong, and he sensed that this was the reason behind his cash flow problems.

Then one year he set up a separate account for his *maaser* money.

"My policy now," he explained, "is that if my job pays me

$50,000 net, I tell myself that I've really earned only $45,000. That 10 percent just doesn't belong to me. It's not my money. It's just been entrusted to me to distribute properly."

He went on, "Today, my budget gets me through the month. Not only that, but the *maaser* is building up quite nicely. Now I only have to sit at my desk and wait for people to come through the door."

**Once, a pot of milk** boiled over in the kitchen of Rav Isser Zalman Meltzer. Rav Isser Zalman had no trouble pinpointing the reason for the event.

"I know exactly why this happened," he said. "This morning, when a poor person came to clean the house, I gave him one coin instead of two. I'm certain that if we were to calculate the exact value of the milk that was lost, we would find that it would be exactly one coin's worth." He then went on to tell the following story.

Rav Chaim of Volozhin was always very scrupulous about giving charity. What's more, he also insisted on giving a fifth instead of a tenth of his earnings. Once, he was in doubt as to whether he had or hadn't given a full fifth. He decided that he would be lenient with himself and assume he had given it.

That day, when a member of his household went to fetch a bucket of water, the bucket fell into the well. When he tried to get the bucket out of the well with an ax, the ax fell in too.

When Reb Chaim was told about what had happened, he added up the cost of the bucket and the ax. It came to the exact amount he had decided not to give to charity. He immediately set aside that amount, and several moments later was told that both bucket and ax had been recovered.

**It's not always the size** of the donation that reveals a person's true nature, either. More often than not, it's the way a *baal habayis* receives a fund-raiser.

Not too long ago, I was at the very end of a trip to the States, and I was really looking forward to getting home. I knocked on a rabbi's door, and he invited me in.

"How are you feeling?" he asked me.

I can't remember what had happened that day, but I do remember that I was in a terrible mood. So I just said, "Terrible."

"How come?"

"I just want to get home to my wife and kids. The kids are waiting for their presents from the States, I'm tired of running around, and it's been a really long trip." I didn't feel too good about taking out my frustrations on him, because he had always been so kind to me in the past. But I was really at the end of my rope.

"If this is the case, why come to me? I only give you ten dollars."

"Your ten dollars is worth more to me than a hundred dollars from someone else," I answered. "Even though their donation means more money for the yeshiva, until they give it to me, *mir ken ois reisen der kishkes*, you can eat your heart out. On the other hand, whenever I come to you, I know I'll get ten dollars, plus a hello, plus a smile and a drink with no problems, no hassles, and then I'm on my way."

A nice story, but it doesn't end there. He then asked for his check back, tore it up, and wrote out a new one for a much larger amount.

"What are you doing?" I said. "That wasn't my intention! I can't take more money from you than you wanted to give in the first place."

I know this man. He's a rabbi. His salary isn't exactly what you would call the highest, and he's got children at home, and another one in Eretz Yisrael to support, too.

Even so, he insisted that I take the check, and that I had no right to refuse his donation to the yeshiva.

**Reb Yudel Holtzman** was one of the more learned residents of Strauss Courtyard in Yerushalayim. He was very scrupulous in his mitzva observance, and many interesting stories have been told about him.

Once, a Yerushalmi tailor needed an expensive operation. It was going to cost sixty lira, a fortune in those days. His only option was to send someone from house to house to collect money for his cause. Naturally, the charity collector went to Reb Yudel's home and told him the tailor's story.

Reb Yudel sighed. "What can I do? I've already given away all of my *tzedaka* money to the many needy people who have come to me. I could say the money I give you will be considered *maaser* of my income for the coming year, as the Noda BiYehuda explains, but I've already done that!"

When the charity collector heard this, he got up and left. Before he had gotten far, he heard Reb Yudel calling, "Come back! Come back!"

Reb Yudel said, "I have to help this tailor. Go and borrow twenty lira from the free loan society, and I'll pay it back at the rate of half a shilling a week."

How had Reb Yudel come up with the figure of half a shilling?

"I sat down and calculated that I spend half a shilling a week on wine for Kiddush. I realized I can make Kiddush on challa, and then I'll have half a shilling with which to repay the loan."

The charity collector followed Reb Yudel's instructions and was able to secure the loan.

Twenty lira in those days was a lot of money. It took Reb Yudel more than sixteen years to pay it all back.

**I enjoy collecting** smaller donations from those who mean well more than I like landing the big money from a *baal* *habayis* who loves to give fund-raisers a hard time. Either way, the end result is the same. The donor who is out to take your time has to be crossed off your list, because if he isn't, you just won't get your job done.

For instance, I used to visit a *baal habayis* who gave generously but always insisted on hearing a *devar Torah* first. And it had to be something elaborate, mind you, not just a cute *vort*. After a collector gave over his *devar Torah*, this *baal habayis* would evaluate it. According to the quality of the *devar Torah*, he would then rate the institution or the individual collector, and write out a check that reflected this rating.

Eventually, I stopped going to him. I felt his method was all wrong. Let him *farher* anyone he wants. If he has the time and money, he can travel around the world testing fund-raisers. For us fund-raisers, though, time is of the essence, especially if we've flown across the Atlantic to raise money. We're in the States for only a limited amount of time, and while we're there, we need to get our job done. If a *baal habayis* wants to talk, even to talk in Torah, the time spent talking is a sacrifice for the fund-raiser and the institution that sent him.

**That particular *baal habayis*** was a good man who meant well. Plenty of others seem like they're just out to drive you crazy. Take the time a former student of the yeshiva took me around his neighborhood back in the States to raise funds. He had repeatedly asked me to come, because he thought the area had potential, and he wanted to help me make some money for the yeshiva. After a few years, I finally got in touch with him and said, "If your offer still stands, I'll be more than happy to take you up on it." We got together and made the rounds. Most of the people were very receptive and generous, and everything was going just fine — until we walked into the home of a certain *baal habayis*.

As soon as we walked in and explained what had brought us there, the man turned to the young man who brought me and asked, "What are you doing here?"

My companion began to repeat the reason for our visit, but the *baal habayis* didn't let him finish. "That's not what I'm asking. I'm asking why you're not in Eretz Yisrael."

"I was in Eretz Yisrael for a few years," he answered, "but I came back to look for a *shidduch*."

The *baal habayis* shot back, "That's not a real reason to leave. You could have found a wife in Eretz Yisrael. All Jews belong in Eretz Yisrael!" He then turned to me and said, "You don't belong here, either. It's amazing that there are actually people who are too lazy to work, so they sit in *kollel*. Then, when the money runs out, they fly to America to pick up some easy bucks by schnorring."

By this time, I had had it with this guy, and I decided to give him a piece of my mind.

"First of all, as far as this young man is concerned, you might be right. He and every other Jew belongs in Eretz Yisrael. However," I said, "that includes you, too. Second, as far as not going to work because of laziness, I want you to know that I have my own business in Eretz Yisrael. I took time off from the business to raise money for the yeshiva in which I learned. Not only that, but even though I have my own business to attend to, I still keep a *seder* at the yeshiva." To sum it up, I said, "When I come to you for a donation, you're not doing *me* a favor, I'm doing *you* a favor." I then told him that if he wanted to give me money for the yeshiva, it was fine with me, and if he didn't, that was okay, too.

Obviously, he wrote out a check for the yeshiva.

After the way he made us feel, I felt like tearing up the check and walking away. Then again, I don't believe a fund-raiser has the right to refuse a donation for his yeshiva. I guess it was just another example of what the Gemara says: *L'fum tzaara agra*, which, loosely translated, means, "The reward you get is proportional to the suffering you go through." To this day, I regret not tearing up his check.

**One of the advantages** of being on the road is gaining the opportunity to meet so many different kinds of people, from the simplest to the greatest. A fund-raiser from the famous Novarodoker Yeshiva went, as he did every year, to make the rounds of his *baalebatim*. When he came to the town of Karlin-Pinsk, he decided to stop at the home of one of the acknowledged *gedolei hador*, the author of the *Beis Dovid*. At this time, the Beis Dovid was very old, in his nineties. Though his memory was failing, he still was able to review *Shas* every day by heart.

When the fund-raiser entered the home of the Beis Dovid, they exchanged greetings. Then the Beis Dovid asked him what he wanted.

"I'm here for my annual donation," said the fund-raiser.

"How much do I give every year?" asked the Beis Dovid.

When he was told the amount, the Beis Dovid handed over the money to the fund-raiser and then went right back to learning the way he usually did — by humming the Gemara to himself from memory.

Unable to tear himself away from the holy scene before him, the fund-raiser pulled up a chair and sat listening to the Beis Dovid as he reviewed the Gemara with its commentaries page by page from memory.

After some time passed, the Beis Dovid greeted the fund-raiser once again and asked what he wanted. The fund-raiser repeated his original answer, but said that he had already received the donation. This happened several times during the Beis Dovid's study session.

Finally, the Beis Dovid remarked, "My memory gets worse from moment to moment, but thank G-d, I still remember all of *Shas* just the way I did when I was a youngster at the age of sixteen."

The fund-raiser was struck by this last statement of the Beis Dovid, and when he next had an opportunity to see the Chofetz Chaim, he told him the story.

Not long afterward, the Beis Dovid passed away. Immediately afterward, the fund-raiser received a telegram from the Chofetz Chaim informing him that eulogies were going to be said in Radin, and asking that the fund-raiser come and tell his story to everyone.

When the fund-raiser arrived in Radin, he said to the Chofetz Chaim, "Who am I to eulogize in the presence of the Chofetz Chaim?"

The tzaddik answered, "You won't. You'll just tell your tale, and I will be the one to give the eulogy."

**There are times** when no matter how hard a fund-raiser tries he just can't get someone to give. I've found that people tend to try to give some reason or excuse as to why they can't give you any money.

I once went to a city for the first time. I didn't have much of a list to work with, but one *baal habayis* actually gave me a twenty-five-dollar donation. That was a nice donation back then.

The next year, I went to his factory, which was a small one, and asked to speak with the boss. He came out and said, "Rabbi, what can I do for you?"

I said, "The first thing you can do for me is give me a seat so that I can talk to you."

He brought me into his office and broke down crying.

"What's the matter?" I asked him.

"Rabbi," he said, "I've given money to others all my life, but now I'm bankrupt. I don't have anything to give you."

You can never judge another person. You never know what's hurting him.

**One year, one of my old donors** told me to call first before coming to see him. In respect of his wishes, I did exactly that. The following year, he kept putting me off. The third year, he told me he couldn't see me at all. I later learned that his business had failed, and that he had declared bankruptcy. He couldn't bring himself to tell me, and that's why you have to respect a person's feelings when they avoid you. You never know what's really going on in their lives.

**Bankruptcy isn't the only** personal issue that can disrupt a person's donations. I used to see a certain *baal habayis* who gave me three hundred dollars the first year, and five hundred dollars every year after that.

One year, he said he just couldn't give anymore. When I asked him why, he said, "My wife gives me a hard time about it."

I said to him, "So don't tell your wife. Aren't you the one making the money?"

He said sadly, "But she looks over the checkbooks. She doesn't let me give away a penny to charity."

**More often than not**, when people tell me they're not in a position to help at that moment, I take it at face value — which reminds me of a story that took place in Russia.

A man was wondering what he should do to avoid the draft. Should he say he was older than he really was, or should he claim that he was younger than he really was? He was stumped and couldn't make up his mind. When a friend came along, he asked the friend what he should say.

"What would happen if you just told the truth?"

What was the man's response? "You know, it never even crossed my mind!"

So I prefer to take people's words at face value instead of always trying to read some deeper meaning into everything — which reminds me of another story:

A rabbi once gave a lecture that lasted about two hours.

Right when he began to speak, a bird flew over and lit on the windowsill. It stood perched there facing the classroom. As soon as the *shiur* was over, it took off.

One of the students approached the rabbi afterward and said with obvious hesitancy, "Rebbe, do you think that maybe...just maybe...the bird might have been a *gilgul* of a person who was reincarnated as a bird?"

The rabbi smiled and answered the question with another question. "Could it have been that maybe...just maybe...it was just a bird?"

# Seeing the Hand of G-d

Rav Chaim of Volozhin was once visited by a businessman who said, "Rebbi, I've got big problems. I sent my ships full of lumber to Prussia, but the border guards won't let them through!"

Rav Chaim said, "Don't worry. G-d will help you."

In the interim, the price of lumber rose dramatically, and the businessman made thousands because of the delay at the border. He went back to Rav Chaim.

"Rebbi, your blessing came true! Now I see the hand of G-d."

"Look at that," mused Rav Chaim. "The poor see the hand of G-d all the time, while the rich only see it once every few years!"

# Seeing the Hand of G-d

In my line of work, you need a lot of *siyatta diShemaya* to deal with all the challenges you have to face. Take the language barrier, for instance. A fund-raiser who knew only a minimal amount English once stepped into an office and asked to see the boss, Mr. Klein. When the secretary told him that Mr. Klein was deceased, the fund-raiser said, "No problem — I'll wait."

Seriously, though, when you travel from one country to another, you need to deal with more than just the language barrier. A fund-raiser has to worry about dealing with the local currency, finding his way around, not getting ripped off, and all the other innumerable problems that come with the territory. Learning the ropes takes years.

**During a fund-raising mission** to Europe, a fundraiser was once traveling by train. He didn't know the language, but he could tell he was nearing his destination, because they had crossed the border. Not knowing exactly what to do, the fund-raiser decided to approach the best-dressed person on the train to ask for help. He figured that someone that well dressed would also be well educated, and would be able to give him the guidance he needed. Their conversation went something like this:

"Excuse me, do you speak English?" asked the fund-raiser.

"Yes, a little," answered the gentleman.

"Could you please tell me how many more stops there are to _____?"

The businessman thought a moment and said, "It is three more stops from here."

Seeing how well things were going, the fund-raiser decided to ask for further assistance. "Do you happen to know where I can cash dollars for local currency there?"

The man answered, "Yes, but the banks are all closed today. It's Sunday."

"What do you suggest I do? I have to go to this town."

The man then switched to Yiddish. "Ihr kumt far a mossad?" (Are you here to raise money for an institution?)

The fund-raiser was floored. "Yes."

The man then handed over a wad of bills in the local currency. Still speaking in Yiddish, he said, "If so, then take this. Consider it my contribution. You'll find that it's more than enough to get you where you're going."

**This same fund-raiser checked** into a hotel in Europe one evening and immediately started to call the *baal habayis* he had come to see. He wasn't successful in getting through to the man and assumed that he had misunderstood the local phone code and wasn't dialing properly. He went down to the lobby to ask one of the clerks for help. When he got there, he gave the place the once-over and decided that the bellboy seemed to be the most understanding of the lot. He went over and explained his predicament.

"Of course you can't reach him," the bellboy answered in Yiddish. "Everyone's at Maariv!"

**Of course,** *siyatta diShemaya* goes far beyond getting past the language barrier.

A *rosh yeshiva* once told a young student that their institution was in desperate need of ten thousand dollars. "Go to a certain city, and raise the money."

This young man hopped on a plane and flew to the city. When he got there, though, he didn't have the faintest idea as to how to go about raising that kind of money. Not knowing where or how to begin, he found his way to the local shul, picked up a Gemara, and started to learn.

As he was learning, two men approached him, gave him a hearty "Shalom aleichem!" and asked him, "What brings you to our town?"

The young man told them his whole story — how his yeshiva desperately needed ten thousand dollars, and that his *rosh yeshiva* had sent him to that very city to raise it. He explained to them that since he didn't know the first thing about raising money, he had made his way over to the shul to learn. At least he would be spending his time in the city doing the job he knew how to do!

As their conversation unfolded, this young man gave the two members of the community a vision of all the yeshiva represented and the kind of work it did. He explained how his *rosh yeshiva* had helped him get off drugs and turn his life around. The men heard him out, and then asked the student to come back to the shul on Shabbos to make an appeal.

That Shabbos, the young man told his entire story in all its moving detail in front of the congregation. Lo and behold, he raised the whole ten thousand dollars!

He called his *rosh yeshiva* the following day and excitedly described all that had happened during the three or four days since his arrival. The *rosh yeshiva* gently suggested that he consider staying another few days, but the student had had enough of fund-raising. He just wanted to get back to his own *shtender* to sit and learn.

**A friend of mine told me** that once, many years ago, he was in Kansas waiting to catch a train to another city. Since he had time on his hands, he decided to go and get his shoes shined. It wound up taking longer than he had expected, and by the time he was finished at the stand, the train to his next stop had already pulled out of the station and was long gone. In those days, fund-raisers didn't just hop onto airplanes. The only thing he could do was wait for the next train (whenever it would show up), or better yet, choose a new destination on the spur of the moment. Being a spontaneous sort of guy, he was out on the very next train.

My friend told me that his unplanned stop was a fund-raising success — and it became clear later that had he gone to his original destination, he would have come back with nothing.

"Missing that train," he said, "was pure *hashgacha pratis*."

**The truth is, every step** one takes is a story of *hashgacha pratis*.

At the beginning of my trip in one city, I went to see a *baal habayis* who was a lawyer by profession. I knocked at his door on a Sunday morning, but he told me right away that it was impossible for him to give me any time.

"There's nothing I can do for you. I have a big case about to go to court, and I have to spend every second of the day preparing for the trial. If you're still in town when it's over, I'll be glad to see you." He then gently, but firmly, closed the door on me.

In my line of work, you just have to keep plugging away. I didn't really think I would get to see him that year, but I figured I would give it one more try before leaving town.

I went back a week later and knocked on his door once again. This time he said, "Please come in. You must have *ruach hakodesh*! Your timing couldn't have been better. I won the case today, and I walked out with a handsome check."

**A fund-raiser once came** to a wealthy businessman for a donation. He said that he was raising money for an institution for the handicapped. The fund-raiser gave a moving talk about the type of child who benefits from their services, and described in detail the sort of backgrounds these children come from.

Suddenly, the potential donor said to himself, *Hey, wait a minute! I've got very close friends and relatives who have handicapped children enrolled in a school like that. If anything, I should really send them a check! I'll give this guy a few bucks, since I don't know him from Adam, and he doesn't even look like a person from my circles, and then I'll send a real check to the people I know.*

Not wanting to be rude, he decided to sit through the rest of the fund-raiser's spiel. As he sat there listening with half an ear and vaguely looking at the pictures and slides, he suddenly spotted his friend with the handicapped child in one of the photos! That clinched the deal. He immediately gave the fund-raiser a sizeable donation. The fund-raiser and the businessman later became very good friends.

**A fund-raiser will sometimes** make an effort to forge a new contact with someone really wealthy. Sometimes, he gets lucky and gets in to see the person right away. Other times, it can take a lot of perseverance and pushing. And then there are times when it borders on the impossible. I personally believe that nothing is really impossible, and that it is just a matter of not giving up — and, of course, a healthy dose of *siyatta diShemaya*.

Once, Rabbi Stern tried to make just such a contact. When he called the man's office, he was told to try him at home. When he called the man's home, he was told to try at the office. This went on for weeks!

Later, Rabbi Stern left Eretz Yisrael on another fund-raising trip via Ben Gurion Airport. Now, when you fly to or from Eretz Yisrael, you have to take a shuttle bus to get from the terminal out to the airplane on the tarmac. The ride is short — two minutes at most — so you don't really get much of a chance to talk during the ride. If you have something to say to someone, it has to be short and to the point.

As Rabbi Stern rode the shuttle from the terminal out to the plane, he spotted the man he had spent weeks trying to contact. The rabbi walked right over to him and said, "G-d has a funny sense of humor, doesn't He?"

**A man known for giving charity** to many causes was once very irritated with a local Torah institution for some reason or another but, as things often go, the institution tried to get a donation out of him anyway. When the fund-raiser went to see the donor in his office, the donor took the opportunity to tell him just how peeved he was with the institution.

While this scene was unfolding, there were two other people standing there who had come to raise money for *hachnasas kalla*. Just to show how angry he really was and to spite the fund-raiser of the local institution, the wealthy donor wrote out checks then and there for the two men who had come from out of town.

The sum of each check was eighteen thousand dollars. Talk about being in the right place at the right time!

**Sometimes the story** of how someone becomes a supporter of a certain institution is so complex, even the major players in it can almost forget how it all began.

In a certain town, there was a couple that got into a huge
fight. As is usual, they dragged the local rabbi into it as well,
with both of them trying to get him to take their side. In such
cases, for some odd reason, no matter which side the rabbi
takes, he's always on the wrong side. Both sides usually wind
up hating the rabbi, and even if he tries to stay out of it, he
somehow ends up in trouble anyway. And that is exactly what
happened in this no-win situation.

Eventually, the couple reconciled their differences, but since
the rabbi had taken sides, they both refused to daven in his shul.
What's worse, they would both go so far as to cross to the other
side of the street whenever either of them saw him coming.
There was another shul in the vicinity, so as far as the rabbi was
concerned, they were welcome to daven there.

Several months after the couple got back together, one *erev
Shabbos* the rabbi spotted the wife walking toward him, looking
as though she was about to burst into tears. She recognized the
rabbi and said, "Rabbi, I don't know where my husband is. He
didn't come home from work yet. I'm very worried about him.
He usually comes home a few hours before Shabbos, but now it's
after candle lighting, and I haven't heard from him. I'm so worried!"

The rabbi tried to calm her. "Listen. Come into the house, sit
down with the rebbetzin, and I'll go talk to the police. We'll see
what we can do."

When it comes to a missing person, the police are usually
willing to get involved only after twenty-four hours have
passed. But the rabbi hoped that they would be willing to call
the office and find out if the husband was still there.

The only response at the office was from the answering
machine, which wasn't any help at all. In the meantime, the wife

was worried sick, and was beginning to get hysterical.

The rabbi explained to her that they had done what they could, and that they now had to have some patience.

"There must be a good reason for this," he told her. "If you want, you can stay with us. The rebbetzin and I will give you your own room, and we'll do whatever we can for you."

The wife, however, wouldn't think of it. "Thank you, Rabbi, but I've got to get back to the kids."

That night at about half past eleven, as the rabbi was heading home from a *shalom zachar*, he saw the missing husband walking down the block, apparently heading for home. The rabbi approached him and asked him what had happened.

"Your wife was looking all over for you," the rabbi said, "and she's a nervous wreck. I think you should come with me to my house first." They walked to the rabbi's house together, and the rebbetzin got up to serve him a full Shabbos meal.

The missing husband explained what had happened.

"I got caught in a branch office near the airport. A water pipe burst, and I had to fix it on the spot. Before I knew it, it was getting close to Shabbos. I was filthy from doing the repair, and I didn't have a change of clothing. I didn't even have a siddur with me. I figured the best thing to do would be to leave my car there and find a non-Jewish taxi driver to take me home. So that's what I did. I kept an eye on the time, and just outside the city limits, I realized I had to get out, because it would be Shabbos any minute. I've been walking ever since."

The rabbi said, "I have to tell you something. I can't let you go home yet. The halacha clearly states that if a person enters a city on Shabbos from outside the city limits, he may not go to his final destination on Shabbos. You won't be able to go home until after Shabbos. You'll have to stay with us until then."

"But Rabbi," he protested, "I don't have any clothing or food!"

"Don't worry," said the rabbi. "We'll take care of everything.

That's why I'm the rabbi. I'm here to help people with their problems."

The rabbi then walked over to the man's house and knocked on the door, waking up the man's wife to tell her the wonderful news. He related all that had happened, that her husband was just a few blocks away, and that he couldn't come home, since he had come from outside the city limits.

"He does, however, need some clothes. I'll put them on and wear them to my house so that I won't be carrying them."

Just imagine this rabbi walking home at two o'clock in the morning wearing a suit two inches too big at the waist with the pants cuffs dragging behind him. The jacket was even worse. It made the rabbi look like a scarecrow. At least there wasn't anyone around to see him.

As he left, he invited the wife over once again to his home, this time so that she could join her husband for Shabbos. She thanked the rabbi, said she was very happy he was home safely, but that she felt she had to stay with the children.

"So bring the children, too," offered the rabbi.

"That's all right. I'll stay home with them. I'm just so happy to know that he's okay," she said.

The couple was so touched by the rabbi's concern and efforts on their behalf that the husband showed up at his shul the next morning. And not only did he come to the shul (which was close to the rabbi's home), he sat right next to the rabbi! When the president of the shul walked in a few minutes later, he did a double take. He couldn't believe he was seeing the two of them together that way.

Over time, this man became one of the rabbi's most vocal and active supporters in the shul.

**I once traveled to see a friend** of mine. I didn't travel for money; I didn't even go to my friend for money. It was purely a social visit. That happens once in a while too, you know. Anyway, as I was sitting in my friend's home, a fundraiser popped in. He saw me and said, "Rabbi, something interesting happened to me today. I ran into someone, and he gave me a hundred dollars. He's a very interesting man. Even if you're not here to raise money, you should still go out to see him."

What should I do, not go? In my line of business, if someone tells you to go and see someone else, you do it. The fact is that I also found the man interesting, and he also gave me a hundred dollars. When I was about to leave, he said to me, "Rabbi, please, please come to see me when you come back to town. Don't forget to come and see me."

The following year, I went to see him again. That year, he gave me $500. The year after that, he gave me $1000. The last time I saw him, he gave me $12,000.

I thought I went to the place for a vacation, but one never knows where Hashem is leading him.

**Once, a very poor man** in Yerushalayim needed to make a wedding for his child. He knew he had to come up with a certain sum, but he had no idea who to turn to.

One day, a friend said, "Why don't you go to a certain yeshiva and just ask them for their mailing list?"

No yeshiva likes to give out its mailing list, but the administrators just didn't have the heart to turn this poor man away. They decided to give him a dead list — in other words, a list of people from whom the yeshiva had solicited funds in the past, but who had never responded with a donation.

The poor man decided that he would write to the people on the list, since he couldn't bear to leave Eretz Yisrael.

After several weeks, just when the man was about to give up hope, he received a check in the mail for eighteen thousand dollars. The envelope contained a letter along with the check that said, "Go ahead with the wedding, and I will take care of any additional expenses."

The man was so thrilled, he ran straight to the yeshiva's office to thank the head administrator.

To say the administrator was surprised would be an understatement. He decided to investigate. What he discovered was this: the *baal habayis* abroad had a daughter who the doctors had diagnosed with cancer. The father pledged that if his daughter had a complete recovery, he would give a large donation to the next person to ask him for charity.

Just as he opened up this poor man's letter, the doctor called to apologize. "The staff switched the samples around somehow. Your daughter isn't sick at all."

**A Jewish soldier** in the American armed forces was once stationed in Panama. In those days, it was hard enough to keep kosher wherever you were, but in the armed forces it was all the more difficult. It didn't make things any easier that this person's commanding officer was a big anti-Semite. To make matters worse, the soldier was about to be transferred to a camp where obtaining kosher food was absolutely impossible. He didn't know where to turn.

At that time, someone told him that the Rav of Kletsk had just arrived in America and strongly recommended that he go see the rav, who was none other than Rav Aharon Kotler.

The first chance he had, the Jewish soldier went to see Reb Aharon and told him his problem.

Reb Aharon told him not to worry. "Everything will work out," he said.

When the soldier returned to base, he discovered that his orders had been changed, and that he was being transferred to the Panama Canal instead. At the Canal, things were much easier, and obtaining kosher food wouldn't be any problem at all. The soldier was so ecstatic that he went out to the community at large and raised one thousand dollars for Reb Aharon.

The **Ponovezher Rav** had just returned to Eretz Yisrael from one of his fund-raising trips to New York. Unfortunately, he hadn't been as successful as he had hoped to be, but he was at least relieved to be back home. When he arrived in Bnei Brak, one of the yeshiva's administrators told him that a wealthy *baal habayis* from South Africa had just arrived. The man wanted to donate a large sum of money to the yeshiva on the condition that his name would be put on the wing he would be financing.

When the Ponovezher Rav heard this, he asked for the name of the *baal habayis*. Upon hearing the man's name, the rav said that it would be impossible to put his name on a wing of the yeshiva, since he wasn't up to par with their standards of religious observance.

The rav said, "Just tell this *baal habayis* that you'll have to speak with me when I come back. I don't want to lie, so until this *baal habayis* goes home, I will return to *chutz laaretz*. If he asks when I will be coming back, tell him that I am abroad, and that you don't know when I will be returning."

On the plane out of Eretz Yisrael, an elderly Jew sat next to the rav. Every few minutes, he shot a look of distaste in the rav's direction. Finally, the Ponovezher Rav asked the man what he had done to deserve that kind of treatment.

The man answered, "I went through the camps, and I struggled all my life to get where I am now. I finally made enough money to visit Eretz Yisrael for the very first time. Before I left New York, I saw you raising money. I saw you while I was in Eretz Yisrael, and now here you are again on my return flight! Where on earth are you getting all this money from?"

The Ponovezher Rav then told the elderly man what had happened with the South African *baal habayis*, and said he was flying back to the States just to be on the safe side and so that he wouldn't be telling a lie.

The elderly man thought a minute and then said, "If that's the case, then here is my name, address and telephone number. Check me out, and if I meet your standards, I'll match this South African's donation, and you can put my name on the building instead of his!"

And that's exactly what happened.

**The former executive director** of a Torah institution once confessed to me that the pressure to raise money when you are in a position of responsibility is unbelievable.

"It was hard enough when the yeshiva I helped found was getting off the ground," he said, "but once it needed land and a building, I didn't know where to turn. Aside from the cost of expansion, we still had to meet the payroll, pay the bills, cover maintenance, and support the *kollel*."

I shook my head sympathetically. The story was a familiar one to me.

"That doesn't even take food and rent into account!" the director exclaimed. "My heart always went out to the *rebbeim*. They'd come to me saying, 'At least give us a postdated check so we can buy food for our families!'

"We'd already done all we could. The poor and the middle class don't have much to give, and the wealthy had been tapped more times than I can tell you."

He told me that while the yeshiva was going through this financial crisis, a local election was going on. One of the candidates was a real cowboy — from the ten-gallon hat to the silver belt buckle, all the way down to his cowboy boots. On the chance that this fellow might win the election, the yeshiva felt it would be a good idea to wine and dine him during the campaign. They invited him down to the yeshiva, and the candidate eagerly accepted their invitation. Not only would it be good public relations, but he needed help distributing his campaign paraphernalia and hoped the yeshiva would agree to lend a hand.

The cowboy with the Texas drawl came on down to the yeshiva, and my friend rolled out the red carpet for him. He showed him all there was to see, saving the *beis medrash* for last. My friend wanted to make it clear that they weren't some cult, but a genuine academic institution. He also didn't want to give his unusual visitor culture shock by exposing him first thing to a *beis medrash* full of students swaying over their Gemaras.

Eventually, they came to the *beis medrash*. When the executive director opened the doors, the cowboy suddenly began to choke up, coughing and hacking away, his eyes streaming with tears.

Before the candidate left, they came to an agreement that a handful of boys would help disperse flyers and bumper stickers for the campaign.

Despite their efforts, the cowboy lost the election. Afterward, however, he returned to the yeshiva and said, "Rabbi, I really appreciate everything you did for me. If there's anything at all I can do for you, please let me know."

Figuring that he didn't have much to lose, my friend told the cowboy then and there exactly what the yeshiva needed: land and a building.

The cowboy thought a minute and said, "Rabbi, I've made it big a few times, and I've fallen on my face a few times. Right now, I'm sitting on a ton of different properties. Take your pick of them and build on it, and I'll foot the whole bill. The only condition I'll make is that I want you to negotiate the best deal you possibly can with the bank."

When my friend asked the unexpected benefactor why he was making that kind of an offer, the man explained.

"You see, Rabbi, I was born in Europe. My parents came here from Russia. When they first landed on these shores, my father opened up a little grocery store in New York, right around the corner from a yeshiva. When I was growing up, my father had some of these here books around," he said, meaning the Gemaras. "When you took me into that study hall, my old memories just made me feel like sobbing."

**A family in Eretz Yisrael** was in dire straits, and it was decided to take up a collection for them. The plan was that people would fan out to raise money in their neighborhoods between Mincha and Maariv on a fast day. Some people ridiculed the coordinator of these efforts, Rabbi Silver.

"For the amount of money we need," said one, "this is not going to work. It's not worth the time."

Rabbi Silver replied, "You're right, but we still have to do our utmost and let G-d take care of the rest."

The day arrived, and everyone bought in a few hundred shekels apiece, which did not even come close to the fifty thousand dollars needed.

It was a hot day, and it took real effort to approach people. Rabbi Green, one of the collectors, received a small contribution from a man who then said, "My father just succeeded in a business deal, and he's looking to give the *maaser* money to a worthy cause. I know you're an honest man, so I'll give you a check from him in a few days."

Rabbi Green thought a check for another few hundred shekel wouldn't hurt, and said thank you. A few days passed, and to his surprise, not only did he get the check, but it was for a few thousand dollars.

**Every year, Rabbi Shultz** went to see Mr. Levy, and every year, he received a contribution to his *kollel* from the wealthy businessman.

One year, he went to see Mr. Levy, only to find he was out of the country.

On his way back to Eretz Yisrael, standing in the baggage

check-in line, Rabbi Shultz spotted Mr. Levy coming off a flight that had just landed.

Going right over to Mr. Levy, Rabbi Shultz told him he had gone to his office, but was told he was out of the country.

On the spot, Mr. Levy peeled off a couple of hundred dollars and gave it to the fund-raiser.

In short, if you're supposed to get it, you will.

**A major yeshiva** had a long-standing tradition of sending out calendars to donors and potential donors. In addition to the regular information usually found on a yearly calendar, these came complete with candle lighting and havdala times for Shabbos and holidays.

One year, the yeshiva debated as to whether to continue this mailing. It was an expensive proposition, and the yeshiva was having a very difficult year.

Finally, the decision was made to keep this practice going, sending to all the people on the list, even though some never responded.

One day, out of the blue, the yeshiva received a check from one of these people. How much was the check? Let's just say, enough to put up their building in Jerusalem.

**A fund-raiser once traveled** to the home of a very wealthy man in South Africa. The journey seemed never-ending, the town was literally in the middle of nowhere, and by the time the fund-raiser arrived, it was almost midnight. Since there weren't any hotels, motels, or anything else in the vicinity, he had the choice of either sleeping on the ground where he stood, or risk waking the family by knocking on their door. Considering his options, he naturally chose the latter.

The *baal habayis* answered the door and asked what he could do for the stranger. The fund-raiser explained why he had come, but the *baal habayis* apologized and said, "I'm sorry, but I never support any institutions." Since it was well past midnight, the fund-raiser asked if he could have a place to say his evening prayers and sleep for the night. The *baal habayis* acquiesced and told him that he was welcome to use the guest bedroom for the night.

Feeling rejected and dejected because of all of his wasted efforts and travel expense, the fund-raiser prayed that night to the melody chanted on Yom Kippur with all the feeling his broken heart could muster.

After the fund-raiser finished praying, the *baal habayis* approached him and said, "The last time I heard that melody was twenty years ago, when my father was still alive. My father always prayed with that melody."

The next morning, as the fund-raiser got ready to leave, the *baal habayis* handed him a check — for $100,000! And that check was only the beginning of better things yet to come.

It just goes to show you, when you're meant to get a donation from a certain *baal habayis*, you'll get it. How and when is up to the One Above, but it always works out in the end.

# The Jewish Heart

Rabbi Yissachar Dov of Belz was once visited by a brokenhearted chassid. When the Rebbe asked the miserable man what ailed him, the chassid lamented, "Rebbe, the Gemara says that a poor man is considered like a dead man."

The Rebbe countered, "Go and look at the wealthy man who is childless. He is also considered like a dead man!"

The chassid said, "But Rebbe, there is a difference. The rich man is dead, but he feels like he's in Gan Eden. The poor man feels like he's in Gehinnom!'

"If that's the case," said the Rebbe as he handed the chassid enough money to put him back on his feet, "let me bring you into Gan Eden."

# The Jewish Heart

J ews have an innate tendency to be charitable (*Sanhedrin* 37), and there are many stories about tzaddikim who felt the pain of the poor, and who tried to get them out of their Gehinnom and into Gan Eden.

Rav Chaim Soloveitchik was one. During all the years Reb Chaim was the rav in Brisk, the community provided for all of his family's needs. Once, while reviewing his outstanding debts, Reb Chaim's supporters discovered that his bill for firewood that year had come to five hundred rubles. They couldn't understand how it could be. Even the wealthiest home owner didn't spend more than fifty rubles a year on firewood!

They did some checking and found out that Reb Chaim's own woodshed was left unlocked, and that the town's poor had made a habit of treating his wood as if it was their own. The communal leaders promptly took care of the situation by locking the shed and giving the key to the shammes.

When Reb Chaim heard what the communal leaders had done, he demanded that the lock be removed immediately. It was, and once again, the poor came and took from the shed as much wood as they needed. When the *parnassim* of the community heard what was going on, they approached Reb Chaim.

"Rabbi, there isn't enough money in the community coffers to provide unlimited free firewood to all the poor of our city!"

"If that's the case," Reb Chaim answered, "then I won't heat my own house, either. How can I sit in a warm home when the poor are freezing?"

**Reb Chaim's hand** was always open to the poor, and if he was temporarily without funds, he didn't hesitate to borrow. As his merits piled up, so did his debts. Once, he was asked how he expected to pay back all the money he owed. He answered, "Here in Brisk, there are a lot of wealthy people. They can repay the money I borrowed to give to the poor!"

Needy people from all over the surrounding countryside knew that Reb Chaim was someone they could turn to. He always gave without reservation, and would remind those who came to him, "Brisk is full of wealthy people. Go to them, too. They should also help you."

Brisk, like many other cities in those days, had an organized group that supported the town's poor Torah scholars. Once, Reb Chaim heard there was a great deal of money in the charity box set aside for this purpose. He called over the person in charge of the fund and reprimanded him. "Don't you know that it is forbidden to leave any money in that box?"

**Rav Menachem Nachum of Chernobyl** devoted his life to the mitzva of *pidyon shevuyim*, liberating Jewish captives. He made frequent visits to donors to raise sums of money, which he would then slip into the pockets of various power brokers for this purpose.

Once, when Rav Menachem Nachum was in Zhitomir, he himself was put into jail on trumped-up charges. A tzaddik who came to visit him quoted the verse, "Hashem said to Avraham: '*Lech lecha* — Go, for yourself, from your land and your homeland and the house of your father.'"

Interpreting the verse, the tzaddik said, "Avraham Avinu, who was renowned for his *hachnasas orchim*, always used to look for ways to improve his service to wayfarers. So Hashem said to him, 'Go away from your land,' meaning, leave your home, Avraham, so that you yourself should become a wanderer, and then you will learn firsthand the needs of a traveler and how you can help him.

"Because you are a great redeemer of captives," concluded the tzaddik, "from heaven you have been given the opportunity to experience captivity yourself. From this experience, you will understand more deeply the urgency of redeeming a Jew from captivity as soon as possible."

**Reb Elya Chaim of Lodz** worked tirelessly on behalf of the community and individual Jews, never hesitating to raise money for those in need. One year, Lodz was blessed with an unusually cold winter. There was snowstorm after snowstorm, the temperatures were at an all-time low, prices were up, the cost of fuel was sky-high and jobs were scarce. That was why Reb Elya Chaim could be seen one evening heading out toward the wealthy side of town, on his way to get money from the wealthier people of Lodz for fuel for the poor

His first stop was the home of the richest of the rich, Reb Kalman Poznansky. The servant who answered the door recognized the esteemed visitor and hastened to welcome him inside.

Reb Elya Chaim, though, indicated that he would wait.

When Reb Kalman heard who was waiting on his doorstep, he hurried to personally invite Reb Elya Chaim inside.

Oddly enough, even after he greeted the rabbi and invited him into his home, Reb Elya Chaim didn't budge from the open doorway. The rabbi began talking about the news of the day and the needs of the poor. Out of respect for the rav, Reb Kalman stood there shivering in his dressing gown while Reb Elya Chaim spoke leisurely about one topic after the other, as if he was sitting comfortably inside a warm study.

Finally, Reb Kalman could stand it no longer. "Rabbi, please come inside the house. I'm freezing!"

Aha! Here was the opportunity Reb Elya Chaim was waiting for. Not budging from his position in the doorway, he said, "I'd like to tell you why I've come to see you. This winter has been unusually harsh, prices are very high, and the poor cannot afford firewood to heat their homes. I'm here to ask for your help."

Reb Kalman was only too happy to contribute.

When they finally entered the house, Reb Kalman asked, "Why was it necessary to wait outside so long before coming in? Is this some sort of custom with which I'm unfamiliar?"

Reb Elya Chaim answered, "A man who has just eaten a sumptuous meal can't possibly understand the agony of those who are hungry. I came to plead on behalf of the poor people who, as we speak, are freezing. Had we sat together in your warm home all this time, you wouldn't have felt even a thousandth of their pain. It's only after standing in the cold for so long that you can begin to appreciate their predicament, and give the way you should."

**On another occasion,** a woman once came crying to Reb Elya Chaim. "Rabbi, my daughter is about to be married, and I'm penniless. My husband died when our daughter was engaged, leaving me a poor widow. I don't know how I can possibly make this wedding!"

Reb Elya Chaim emptied his pockets and looked through the drawers, but no money was to be found in the house. He went into the next room, and returned with two silver candlesticks in his hands.

"Please take these and pawn them," he said to the distraught woman. "Then bring me the receipt."

The woman was reluctant. "Oh, I couldn't do such a thing to you."

Reb Elya Chaim answered calmly, "Please do as I ask. Your daughter has to get married."

That gentle reminder convinced the woman, and she left to pawn the silver candlesticks.

The following *erev Shabbos*, when the rebbetzin was ready to light candles, she couldn't find the candlesticks. After searching high and low, she came to the conclusion that they had been stolen.

Upset, she ran to her husband's study to tell him about the theft.

"Don't worry," said Reb Elya Chaim. "Our candlesticks were privileged to be a part of the great mitzva of *hachnasas kalla*."

"Then how do you propose that I light my candles?" asked the rebbetzin, to which Reb Chaim replied, "Do you mean to tell me that there aren't any potatoes left in the house?" (In those days, poor people would hollow out a potato, full the hole with oil, add a wick and use this for Shabbos candles.)

**When Rabbi Simcha Bunim of Peshischa** was a youngster in the town of Bendin, a poor chassid came to raise money for an even poorer bride. Reb Simcha Bunim gave him a respectable sum, and then told his friend who was in charge of the community's book fund, "Give this man a donation out of the charity box you're in charge of."

When word got out, the *beis medrash* was filled with the voices of people railing at them for stealing from charity money. "You can't take from the book fund to pay for some bride's wedding!"

The townspeople gathered to decide what should be done, and how to prevent it from happening again. Reb Simcha Bunim was at the meeting, and he opened the discussion. Each person present gave his opinion as to why it had been wrong.

Finally, it was Reb Simcha Bunim's turn to speak. He said, "I want to tell you a story.

"Once, there was a plague in the forest. Thousands and thousands of animals were dying, so all of the animals came to the lion, the king of the jungle, to find out how to stop the plague. The lion declared that a plague doesn't come unless some sin has been committed. So the lion and his officers set up a court to determine what sins had brought on the terrible epidemic.

"'Whoever sinned,' declared the lion, 'will be put to death. That way, this plague will stop.'

"The leopard came first to confess. 'Once, I was very hungry. I saw a man, and I killed him so that I could get something to eat.'

"The court decided that the leopard had acted reasonably. He killed only so that he could eat.

"Then the wolf came forward. 'One day, I was as hungry as a dog. I hadn't eaten the entire day. That evening, I saw a cow and her calf. I killed them both and ate them.'

"The court found that the wolf had been justified, too.

"All the other predators came forward as well, and they all had similar stories. The court found them all innocent. The very last animal to speak up was the sheep.

"'One year, it was very cold, so my master had pity on me and brought me into his house. That night, I saw straw in his shoes. Since I was very hungry, I ate it. The next morning, when my master went to the market, he didn't have any straw to fill his shoes.'

"'You are the guilty one!' cried the court. 'It is your fault that the plague began!' And they killed him on the spot.

"We have the very same story here," said Reb Simcha Bunim. "You, Reb Aryeh (Mr. Lion), lent money with interest. But you have no sin on your conscience! And you, Reb Zev (Mr. Wolf), you cheated with your weights and measures. And you, Reb Ber (Mr. Bear), you've cheated your employees out of their wages. But does anyone point the finger at you? No! But this young man, the one in charge of the charity box, who is as innocent as the sheep…"

There was no need for him to continue.

**In the same vein,** Rav Yisrael Salanter once gave a strong verbal rebuke to the people of his town. They had not paid the local Talmud Torah tuition for an orphan who had since taken to walking the streets. They tried to excuse themselves, claiming they did not have the money to pay. He shouted back, "Then sell a *sefer Torah* to pay his tuition."

**Once, Rav Chaim of Sanz** rebuked a certain rav, demanding to know why he showed no consideration toward a certain man who lived in the rav's city whose poverty was such that his family often went hungry.

The rav responded, "I must confess that I was completely unaware of his situation."

Rav Chaim was shocked. "Is that an excuse, to say, 'I didn't know?' That's what Bilaam said to the angel: 'I sinned because I didn't know' (*Bamidbar* 22:34). But if he didn't know, how could he have sinned? Therefore, we see that ignorance itself is a sin.

"The same applies to a communal leader. Both he and the rav must know the plight of the poor. They must be aware of any injustice suffered by anyone in their town. They must be ready to help and support all such people."

**One of the marks of greatness** is a person's willingness to do whatever is necessary to take care of the needs of others. And just as people have many different kinds of needs, the ways in which they can be helped are just as diverse.

Once, Reb Pesach of Lipsik walked into the *beis medrash* to daven Mincha. While he was there, he saw a baker who looked downhearted. He called the baker over and asked him what was on his mind.

"Rebbe," the man said, "today was market day, and I didn't sell a single loaf!"

Reb Pesach told him, "Bring everything to my house." He paid the baker for all his wares, and then took the bread and divided it among the poor.

**When Rav Yisrael Salanter** traveled to Kovno, there was an inn there where the poor people could get a bed. Unfortunately, times were bad and people also slept on the floor. Although the *gabbaim* wanted to improve the place, they couldn't — the communal coffers were empty.

What did Reb Yisrael do? He picked himself up and moved to that inn.

He slept there just one night, because by the morning the entire town was up in arms that Reb Yisrael had slept in such a hovel. The townspeople fixed up the place that very day.

**Giving money to the poor** is more than just a question of dollars and cents. Often, the way we give makes the biggest difference. Reb Yosef Rivlin, one of the pillars of old

Yerushalayim, was walking in the shuk of Meah Shearim one Friday when he noticed a woman crying.

"I lost my money," she wailed. "How will I support myself this month?"

Reb Yosef made inquiries about her, and was told that she received a disbursement from the charity fund each month to the tune of one gold napoleon. To her dismay, she had lost the precious coin.

Reb Yosef took out a gold napoleon from his own pocket, approached the woman, and offered it to her, saying that he had found it. Her eyes lit up. She took the money, thanked him profusely, and ran to purchase her Shabbos food.

Later, people asked him why he had pretended to have found the coin, instead of handing it to her as a donation.

"Had I given it to her," he answered, "she would still have felt bad about having lost her money, and she would have worried about it. This way, I gave it to her, and she didn't feel the loss of her own at all."

**There are even times** when giving can mean going against your principles for the sake of helping another Jew. Reb Nachumke of Horodna, in his modesty and humility, never allowed his portrait to be painted. Once, a Jew came to see Reb Leib, the *moreh horaah* of Horodna, and said, "I don't have any money and I don't have any food. There is only one hope that I have — I know how to paint a little. If Reb Nachumke will let me paint his likeness, I'll be able to sell copies and earn a few pence."

Reb Leib went to Reb Nachumke and told him about the man's request.

Without a moment's hesitation the tzaddik answered, "There is no greater mitzva than helping another Jew who is in trouble." So, despite his original reservations, Reb Nachumke had his portrait painted. When he saw the finished product, Reb Nachumke smiled sadly and said, "What a pity you wasted your time! I don't believe anyone would give you as much as a penny for it."

When the artist took out the portraits to sell, everyone wanted to buy one. They all felt that having Reb Nachumke's likeness hang on the wall of their home would add a touch of sanctity and grandeur. In this way, the artist was able to get back on his feet and become self-sufficient again.

**Rav Yechezkel Landau,** Rav of Prague and author of *Noda BiYehuda*, would daven before the *amud* every year for Ne'ila. Despite the fact that he was not expert in the traditional melodies, the leaders of the *kehilla* felt that Prague's tradition should be upheld, namely, that the rav of the city daven at the *amud* for Ne'ila.

Among the daveners was a beggar. This man listened very carefully to the rav's rendition of the words *"mechalkeil chaim bechessed."* The next day, when he resumed his rounds of knocking on doors for *tzedaka*, he repeated the words of the rav, successfully imitating both the rav's melody and tone of voice. The people enjoyed his imitation and gave more generously than before. The leaders of the *kehilla*, however, saw in the beggar's behavior a lack of respect for the rav of the city, and informed him that if he did not stop his imitation, they would expel him from the city.

Distraught, the beggar came before Rav Landau and explained his situation. He added that he never meant to mock or insult the rav. Rather, he wanted to make the people happy, and in so doing, get a bigger donation.

Not only was Rav Landau not angry or offended, he actually wrote a letter granting the beggar formal permission to use his melody for *mechalkeil chaim bechessed.*

**Rav Meir Shapira** of Lublin was very generous with his own money when it came to giving to the needy.

At the same time, his wife was very frugal when it came to

household spending. She used to say, "If I'm not frugal, how will Reb Meir have the money to give to the poor?"

**Shimon Caftan** was counted among the simple folk of Vilna. He spent his entire life, from sunrise to sunset, raising money for the poor. Whether the rain poured or the snow fell, whether it was blisteringly hot or bitingly cold, you could always hear Shimon Caftan heading your way. He would call, "*Yiddelach*! Please give *tzedaka*!"

Everyone in Vilna, Jew and non-Jew alike, knew Shimon Caftan, and everyone put what they could into his charity box. Shimon Caftan suffered a lot. Yet he refused to take any money for himself from the funds he collected, preferring instead to get by on dry bread. He wore an old caftan summer and winter, and lived in a dark, dank cellar. Whenever a person dropped money into his *pushka*, he would turn away so that he wouldn't see who was giving what.

**Shimon Caftan's way** of maintaining the dignity of those who give is even more necessary when it comes to those who take. Once, the richest man in town fell on hard times. He went to the rabbi of the town and said, "Rabbi, my situation is awful. I need ten thousand rubles to get on my feet again."

The rabbi took it upon himself to raise the funds. He went to several other wealthy people in the town, and one of them said, "Rabbi, I can give you the entire sum right now. Who's it for?"

The rabbi apologized, but insisted on keeping the strictest confidentiality. After several such offers, the rich man saw that the rabbi still refused to divulge the recipient's identity.

The rich man finally broke down. "Rabbi, I see that you're an honest man. I have also fallen on hard times, but I was afraid to say anything for fear that others would discover my secret. But now that I see you can be trusted, you must know, I need help just as badly as he does."

**The ideal way** to give *tzedaka* is, of course, to not tell the recipient that you are giving him *tzedaka*. People have come up with all sorts of ways to accomplish this goal.

In one New York neighborhood, a man who wanted to go into business went to a friend to borrow three thousand dollars. The friend had plenty of money, and it wasn't any problem for him to furnish the loan. When the borrower finally scraped the three thousand together to repay the loan, his friend refused to accept the money.

"I also needed money once," he said, "and someone gave me three thousand dollars. When I tried to repay it, I was told that he had also borrowed the money from someone else. When the time had come for him to repay, his friend had said, 'Hold on to it until someone asks you for a loan.' That is how the money came to my hands, and now it's your turn to do the same thing. Pass it on."

**Reb Elya of Kiatinga** was once strolling along the river's edge when he spotted a man crying.

"Why are you crying?" Reb Elya asked.

The man answered bitterly, "I'm in big trouble. I've been out of work for a long time, and now I'm out of money, too. Just yesterday, a lumber exporter hired me. He gave me 150 rubles to pay for provisions for the trip, and I lost the money! What can I do now? How can I go back to him? He'll think I'm a thief!"

Reb Elya tried to console him. "Don't worry." He took one hundred and fifty 150 rubles out of his pocket and handed it to the astonished man.

Money in hand, the man cheered up considerably. "Who are you?" he asked.

"What difference does it make?" Reb Elya evaded the question.

"Well, I need to know who I have to repay."

"Oh, no," said Reb Elya. "This money is set aside for people in need. The next time you encounter someone who needs help, just pass it on."

**There used to be a cemetery** in Morocco that, like other cemeteries, had a charity box at the front gate. What was unusual about this one was that people were permitted to do one of two things with it, depending on their means. If a person had money, he put money in. And if he didn't have money, he was free to take some out.

And don't think that such things are reserved for little villages out at the other end of the earth. There was a neighborhood on the East Coast that had an interesting custom. Whenever people were sitting shiva, they would receive an envelope that contained a few hundred dollars in cash. If they had what to give, they would place some money into the envelope. If they didn't, they were free to take part of the money in the envelope or all of it, no questions asked.

**Reb Zalman, the son of Reb Uri,** was one of the pillars of the Jewish community of Vilna. He was famous for his Torah knowledge, and for his kindness. One of the acts of *chessed* for which people knew of him far and wide was his willingness to loan people money. All his loans were given interest free, and he had no problem with people who needed to pay the money back slowly.

A person once came to borrow three hundred rubles from Reb Zalman for a period of ninety days.

"I have a business deal, and three hundred rubles is all I need to close it," said the man.

Reb Zalman had never met the man before, so he naturally asked, "Do you have any guarantors?"

The man was crestfallen. "No."

Reb Zalman shook his head. "I'm sorry, but I can't give you a loan without any guarantors."

The man's face fell. Shoulders slumped, he turned around to leave.

"Are you sure there's no one in town you know who can sign for you?" Reb Zalman asked again, sensitive to the pain the stranger was feeling.

Once again, the man shook his head. "The only one in town who knows me is G-d."

"Oh, in that case, there isn't any better guarantor," said Reb Zalman cheerily. He took out a piece of paper and wrote, "G-d is the guarantor," and filed it away with the rest of his papers. He then handed the man the three hundred rubles with his blessing.

Ninety days later, the man returned and said, "G-d was good to me, and my business venture succeeded. Now I want to pay back my loan."

"I'm sorry," said Reb Zalman, "but your loan has already been repaid. G-d has taken care of it."

The man didn't want to hear it, though. He wanted to pay back the loan. Finally, they both agreed that the money would be held in trust by Reb Zalman and used for giving out interest-free loans. They would call the fund after both of their names.

**Whenever a couple** would honor Reb Nachumke of Horodna by asking him to be the *sandak* at a bris, he would inquire into the family's financial state. If they were strapped for funds, he would provide them with whatever they needed to support the mother and new baby during the first week.

Once, a grocer asked Reb Nachumke to be the *sandak* at his son's bris. As was his wont, Reb Nachumke checked out the man's means and found that, although normally he was financially stable, he was having a hard time just then. Reb Nachumke knew there would be a problem, though. The man was unwilling to accept charity in any form. What should he do?

Reb Nachumke approached the new father and asked, "When will you be going to Warsaw?"

"What business have you got in Warsaw, Rebbi?"

Reb Nachumke answered, "I have an acquaintance laid up in the hospital there, and I would like to send him thirty rubles. I don't know his exact address, so I'm hesitant to send it through the post. Do me a favor and please take the money. The next time you go to Warsaw on business, just drop it off at his place."

"But Rebbe, I don't know when I'll be going to Warsaw next."

"That's no problem," answered Reb Nachumke. "Whenever you get around to it will be fine. There's nothing pressing about it. In fact, you can use the money until you get a chance to go. Just take the money from me until then."

The grocer took the money, and in the interim, used it for his wife and baby's needs.

At the bris, the father said, "Rebbe, you didn't tell me the name of your friend in Warsaw."

"It doesn't come to mind right now," Reb Nachumke answered. "It's written down in my book at home."

Afterward, whenever they would meet, the grocer would ask Reb Nachumke for the name. Reb Nachumke would always have some excuse to answer for his never having it with him. After a time, the grocer got back on his feet and repaid the loan.

**One of the functions** of the *kollelim* in the Old Yishuv was to distribute the money that had been sent by Jews in the Diaspora to support the poor of Yerushalayim. Every Thursday, they doled out the money. Some of the regulars who came were extremely poor, and would often come again to draw off of the coming week's allotment so that they could feed their little ones.

One of the Yerushalmi *gabbaim* would come to distribute

money on Friday as well as Thursday, to insure that anyone who couldn't make it on Thursday would have another chance to pick up the much-needed cash.

One Friday, a young married man came to ask for money. The *gabbai* checked his list and asked, "Didn't you already receive your money?"

The young man grew very agitated. He insulted the *gabbai*, and then proceeded to smack him in the face!

Without missing a beat, the *gabbai* instructed his assistant to go into the street right away and get the young man a loan of half a napoleon.

In no time at all, the assistant returned with the money in hand, which was a considerable sum in those days. The *gabbai* gave the money to the young man, and gently wished him a good Shabbos.

The assistant didn't know what to make of what had happened.

Sensing his confusion, the *gabbai* said softly, "If the young man felt compelled to do something that extreme, he must really be in trouble."

**Rav Nosson Tzvi Finkel,** the Alter of Slobodka, would show extra concern for the poor who knocked on his door, and even more so for the handicapped and others whose lot was bitter. He would greet them cheerfully, encourage them and accompany them on their way.

Rav Noach Paley related that once, as he was taking leave of the Alter, the latter asked him, "What will you do if, just as you arrive at your home and are greeted by your whole family, a poor ugly man approaches you for help? You'll surely be upset that precisely at this moment this man has come to bother you, and in your great generosity, you'll give him something to get rid of him.

"But this is not what halacha requires of us. It states, 'Bring home the poor,' and *Chazal* say that 'the poor should be members of your household.' Precisely when you are rejoicing with your family, this is when you should see the poor as members of your family and greet them with joy.

"Moreover, you should give the poor even more attention, and treat them with love and warmth, because while you will see your own family whenever you return home, who knows whether you'll have the opportunity to meet these poor people again in your life?"

**When Rav Eliyahu Chaim Meisels,** the Rav of Lodz, was Rabbi of Prozin, he would sometimes go out to the surrounding towns to raise money for the poor. He always took his own linen with him, since he was very particular about not using anyone else's. Once, as he was coming into a town, the residents met him and told him that a poor bride was getting married right then.

"Now that we have the pleasure of having a rabbi among us, please come and join the festivities!"

Reb Chaim assented.

In the evening, everyone came together at the wedding. The tables were set, the food was ready, yet the bride was still not being brought to the *chuppa*. Reb Elya Chaim asked one of the townspeople what was going on, and was told that the groom refused to go through with the ceremony unless the bride's family agreed to supply linens together with the rest of the dowry. Since the bride's family wasn't in a position to provide linens, the wedding wasn't going forward.

Reb Elya Chaim told this resident of the town to follow him. Together, they removed Reb Elya Chaim's linens from the wagon and brought them to the bride's father.

"Take them, give them to the groom," said Reb Elya Chaim, "and marry off your daughter."

That night, the wedding took place amid great rejoicing.

The next morning, the wagon driver noticed that Reb Elya Chaim's linen was missing.

"Rabbi!" he exclaimed. "Your bedding is missing. It must have been stolen during the night."

"Don't worry about it," the rabbi said. "Let's be on our way."

When they arrived back in Prozin, the driver told the rebbetzin about the theft. She felt very bad about it, but didn't say anything to the rabbi. After Shabbos, Reb Elya Chaim ate *melave malka* as always, and spoke about Torah and the issues of the day. The rebbetzin sat listening to his words. He related what had happened at the wedding, how it had been held up just because of some linens.

At this point, the rebbetzin interjected, "What a pity you didn't give your linens to the bride to save her from such humiliation! Instead, they were stolen."

Reb Chaim smiled. "Do you really believe that I did anything less? I went out there to help the poor, didn't I?"

# It's How You Give That Counts

When the Torah Ohr Seminary was first being built and the shell was already standing, I once brought in a *baal habayis* to meet with the *rosh yeshiva*. After I showed him around, and the *rosh yeshiva* explained the situation, the man took out a book of traveler's checks to give his donation. Every time the man made a move to put the checkbook away, the *rosh yeshiva* would say, "But we need more money for this."

After going through the same routine several times, the *baal habayis* finally laughed and said, "Okay, Rabbi, you win. Just take the whole checkbook!"

# It's How You Give
# That Counts

**R**eb Yitzchak used to work for the Chofetz Chaim Yeshiva. Not the one in Queens and not the one in Eretz Yisrael. Not even the one in Williamsburg, but rather the original: the Chofetz Chaim Yeshiva in Radin. Reb Yitzchak used to travel to South America to raise funds, and the trip would usually take approximately three months, not because he was a schlepper, but because in those days there were no jets, and the only way to go then was by boat.

While in South America, Reb Yitzchak met a friend who was a *landsman* from the shtetl. When asked what he was doing there, Reb Yitzchak explained that he was there raising funds for the Chofetz Chaim Yeshiva on behalf of the Chofetz Chaim himself.

The other person said that he had one coin in his pocket and with that he was planning to buy breakfast, but since he had heard about the great Chofetz Chaim, he would forego his breakfast, and he gave the coin to Reb Yitzchak.

When Reb Yitzchak finally returned to Radin, he gave over all of the money to the Chofetz Chaim, and then took out this coin and handed it to him while relating the story.

The Chofetz Chaim took the coin in his fingers and said, "I don't know what to do with this coin. What should I apply it to? If a person could give up his breakfast so that someone could sit and learn, can you imagine what kind of *kedusha* there is here?"

**In the late 1800s,** Jerusalem was beset by a famine so harsh that people died of starvation in the streets with no one to bury them. The trustees of Kollel Polin sent an urgent telegram to the Rabbi Meir Baal Haness charity fund in Warsaw, which was headed at that time by Rabbi Chaim Eliezer Wachs.

Rabbi Wachs was the Rav of Kalish and later of Piotrokow. He had visited Eretz Yisrael several years before the famine and had written a book, *Nefesh Chaim*, about the need to support Jews there.

Rabbi Wachs called his assistant, Rabbi Paltiel, who was skilled in fund-raising, and showed him the telegram.

Rabbi Paltiel, a Torah scholar of note and dedicated to public service, immediately set out on an emergency fund-raising mission. He began with the most affluent members of the local community, and then decided to travel to a nearby village that was owned by one wealthy Jew.

Rabbi Paltiel showed the rich landowner the telegram and explained the desperate situation. He hoped to receive a generous donation from the man, a hundred rubles or so, two hundred at the most. To his surprise, the man instead asked, "How much will the whole thing cost?"

"At least ten thousand rubles," Rabbi Paltiel replied. "We will need to hire a boat and load it with sacks of flour, rice, beans, potatoes and other foodstuffs."

"I am willing to give you the entire amount," the rich landowner declared, to Rabbi Paltiel's astonishment. "However, in exchange, Rabbi Wachs must sell me his entire portion in the World to Come. It must be a legal sale in a *beis din* with witnesses."

Rabbi Paltiel was taken aback. Under ordinary circumstances, he might have dismissed the proposal out of hand. Given the desperate situation, though, he told the wealthy landowner he would ask Rabbi Wachs and return with an answer.

Rabbi Wachs was so anxious to help the poor of the Jerusalem that he immediately agreed to the proposal, no questions asked.

The rich man kept his side of the bargain. He handed over a small fortune, and a boat loaded with food was soon on its way to Eretz Yisrael.

When the supplies reached Jerusalem, each *kollel* family got a generous share of the basic foodstuffs. Whatever remained after this was distributed to members of the other *kollelim* in the city, and so the people of Jerusalem were saved from starvation.

**Giving to Eretz Yisrael** ranks high on the list of charity priorities. Rav Meir Auerbach was the rabbi of Kalish from 1856 until his departure for Eretz Israel in 1860. During those years, he would go from city to city raising money for Eretz Yisrael.

In one town, the rav attempted to convince Rav Auerbach not to go out collecting. Assuming that the rav felt uncomfortable about accompanying him and having to ask wealthy community members for donations, Rav Auerbach said, "If you are embarrassed, I can go alone."

"Not at all!" exclaimed the rav of the city. "It's because I'm concerned about your honor that I don't want you to go. It doesn't seem right for one of the *gedolei hador* to go knocking on doors for a few pennies."

"There is no shame in this," replied Rav Auerbach. "For Eretz Yisrael, every penny is important."

**On one of Rav Auerbach's visits** to Eretz Yisrael, Rav Yosef Chaim Zonnenfeld, who was still quite young at the time, visited him and asked to buy a copy of his book *Nefesh Chaya*. When he asked the price, Rav Auerbach answered, "This book costs two napoleons. One napoleon is for the author, and the other is for the Yishuv in Eretz Yisrael. I'm prepared to forgo my share, but not the other. Therefore, the book will cost you only one napoleon."

**People who enjoy giving** will always find a good reason why they should give charity to certain organizations. In this spirit, one *baal habayis* made a commitment that if his hometown team won the World Series, he'd give five thousand dollars.

As the end of the series approached, with the game going into the bottom of the ninth and the *baal habayis* hometown team in the lead, two people sitting in a car parked outside listened to the game. As soon as the home team won, these two were knocking on the door.

When the *baal habayis* answered the door, they said, "Five thousand dollars, please."

They got it on the spot.

**There was a certain *baal habayis*** whom I would visit, and we would always sit around to schmooze a bit. Every year, we went through the same routine. He would always ask me, "Rabbi, how much did I give you last year?" and I would always answer, "Not enough, not enough."

"Come on, Rabbi," he would say. "Tell me what I gave you last year."

I would answer, "Not enough. You know exactly how much you gave last year. If you're asking me how much it was, all I can say is that it just wasn't enough. You gave me," and I would insert an amount that was less than what he had actually given me.

"But I gave you five hundred dollars!" he would exclaim.

"I don't believe it," I would retort coolly. "It can't be."

He would then say, "Take out your book for last year and see for yourself."

Naturally, he would be right about the amount. And that year, he would raise the amount to six hundred dollars.

Every year we went through the same routine, and every year he gave me a raise. He knew what he had given, but we always played the same old game. He enjoyed giving and wanted to savor every minute.

**A father told me** that he had once gone through a difficult period financially. At the time, he found himself unable to pay the full tuition for his children's schooling. Naturally, he went to the school and explained his situation to them. They asked to see his tax return, which he readily provided. The administrators then gave him the third degree, which he felt was degrading and dehumanizing. In the end, he got the scholarship for his children, a savings of five thousand dollars.

That Rosh Hashana, the father prayed (in addition to all his other requests) that he should merit making enough money to pay the tuition in full.

"Forget the suits, forget the vacations, forget the luxuries! We can live without all that," he pleaded. "The most important thing is that we should be able to pay the full tuition and not have to suffer any more embarrassment."

That year, the father was fortunate and received a $7500 bonus. Well, there are plenty of things a person can do with that kind of money, but what this man did was write out a check for the entire amount to his children's school and go to meet with an administrator.

The father told the administrator that he would like to pay back the scholarship money. It turned out this was easier said than done. The administrator insisted that his children had received the scholarship fair and square, and that there was no reason whatsoever to repay it.

The father was unwilling to accept that, and he insisted on giving the full amount as a donation to the school. When he handed the check to the administrator, the man nearly fell out of his chair.

"How would you like to apply the money?" the administrator asked, still in shock.

"I really don't care," answered the father.

He was offered a plaque, and took two. Since there was still a few thousand dollars remaining in the balance, it was suggested that he apply the money to the upcoming raffle the school was planning.

Several weeks later, the school called to tell the father that he had won the raffle. What was the prize?

Seven thousand five hundred dollars.

And that isn't even the end of the story. This father told me that ever since, he has been keeping records. During this time, he has been giving 20 percent of his income to charity — and he has always gotten the same amount back in one form or another!

**Once, I went to raise money** in a certain city and I came to one of the houses on my route. The woman of the house answered my knock, but apologized that her husband wasn't home.

"Wait a minute," she said.

She went into an adjoining room, talking to me all the while, and I could hear faint, clinking noises in the background. She emerged from the other room a few minutes later, her hands filled with coins. She apologized yet again and said, "Please take what I managed to gather up from the other room," and dropped it all into my hands.

It was ten dollars in quarters.

**Another *baal habayis*** told me one year that he would appreciate it if I didn't stop by for a check, since the year had been a virtual financial disaster. Later, when I saw him in shul, he told me that he still wanted to have a share in the mitzva. He took a quarter out of his pocket and said, "You may need to buy a cup of coffee while you're on the road, so take the twenty-five cents. The truth his," he went on, "twenty-five cents is sometimes so valuable to me, I would buy it for ten dollars."

I took the quarter and then asked him if he wanted to buy it for ten dollars.

**I think the reason** you find people so willing to give is that they truly understand that giving is a privilege that not everyone gets to claim.

I once went to a Midwestern city just to meet with one businessman. When I got there, I called the man, but his secretary told me he was out of town. A mutual acquaintance had given me this man's name and number, and had asked me to deliver a message. So I asked the secretary when her boss was supposed to return. She said he would be back late the following day.

I figured, if I've got to stay here the entire day, I should at least try to get something accomplished in the meantime. I went over to the rabbi of the community, a man I've known for many years, and I asked him for the names of two powerful players in the city, people who would give something substantial. I wasn't asking him to divulge any secret names. I just wanted the names of two regular people who would be generous.

I walked into the first one cold, without calling first. He listened to my story, and when I finished, he said, "Sorry, I'm not interested."

I walked into the second man's office. He also sat me down and listened to my story. When I finished, he handed me a thousand dollars.

I went back to the rabbi, and he asked, "*Nu?* How did you make out?"

I said, "Well, the second man gave me a thousand dollars."

He was surprised. "Rabbi, you're a miracle worker! He gave you a thousand dollars for the yeshiva? You're a real miracle worker."

I shrugged it off. "If I'm a miracle worker, why didn't the first man give me something, too?"

The rabbi answered, "Today, it was destined that your institution would make one thousand dollars."

"Fine," I said. "Why then wasn't the money split into five hundred and five hundred? Or even seven hundred and three hundred? Why did one person have to give the entire sum?"

The answer was that though neither of the potential donors was yeshiva oriented or even observant, one had some merit that enabled him to give. The other one just didn't.

**A certain rabbi** once told me a story that illustrates this point:

"I had a big donor who wanted me to meet a nonbeliever in his home, in the hopes that I would be able to bring the person closer to his heritage. When I arrived, this nonbeliever said to me, 'Rabbi, how can you take money from my cousin? He doesn't share your beliefs at all!'

"I told her that he's not doing me a favor when he gives me money. I'm doing him a favor. He's a friend of mine, and I like him. I want to give him the gift of doing something for the sake of the Torah."

**My friend Rabbi B.** once went into a store to see someone. As he was waiting, the store owner came over to speak with him.

"Rabbi, whenever a fund-raiser came into my store in the past, I always gave him something. Sometimes I gave more, sometimes less, but I would never turn a person down completely. But lately they've all become so impatient. I can be in the middle of talking to a customer, and they just don't let me finish with him. So, yesterday, I made up my mind once and for all. I'm not going to give another dime to any fund-raisers that come around.

"Today, about an hour ago, a fund-raiser walked into the store. He waited until I finished talking to a customer. Then he asked me, 'Can I speak to the boss?' I told him, 'The boss isn't here.' The fund-raiser gave me a good look and said, 'Do you really think that it pays to give your business away because of two dollars?'

The store owner took a breath and went on. "When he said that, it took me back forty or fifty years. Even though two dollars went a lot further in those days, and I vaguely remembered this being a figure of speech back then. People would give two dollars to a fund-raiser, and it was considered a very nice donation. I looked back at him, took out two dollars, and gave it to him. Right then and there, I decided that I've got to give everyone who comes in. It's a privilege to give your money to support the Torah. You have to have that privilege."

**But what happens** if you don't have that privilege?

Reb Hillel of Amshinov once went to a wealthy man to raise money for the ransom of captives, but was turned away.

A few days later, the rich man's cow broke into a non-Jew's field and wreaked havoc. When Reb Hillel heard about this, he smiled and said, "If a person is worthy, he uses his money to redeem a Jew. If not, he winds up having to spend his money redeeming an ox."

**Rav Elchanan Wasserman,** *rosh yeshiva* of Yeshiva Ohel Torah in Baranowitz, once went on a fund-raising mission to the States. At one of the synagogues where he stopped, he was permitted to make an appeal. He stood up and spoke, proposing that those present who could afford to do so should assume financial responsibility for the yeshiva either for a week or for a day, one day costing eighty dollars. Whoever accepted upon himself such a donation, Rav Elchanan assured the group, would in essence be acquiring for himself the merit of the learning of hundreds of *bachurim* for an entire day or week.

His words had a great effect. A palpable sense of excitement was felt among those present, and it seemed as though he would reap a great response. Just then, however, the rav of the shul approached the podium and asked if he could put in some closing words. The rav proceeded to speak for fifteen minutes on an entirely different subject, weakening the powerful impression Rav Elchanan had made. Then, he launched into the subject of money, only in a different way.

"Every dollar given to the yeshiva is sacred, even one single dollar," said the rav, repeatedly emphasizing the importance of one dollar, as opposed to the eighty dollars about which Rav Elchanan had spoken. As a result, the sum collected from the congregation was insultingly small.

Later in the evening, the rabbi went to visit Reb Elchonon at the home in which he was staying and tried to apologize.

"You probably bear a grudge against me for the small response," the rabbi said.

To the surprise of those present, Rav Elchanan smiled and said, "A grudge? For what? This week, we read in the Torah about building the *Mishkan*, where it says, 'I have called by name Betzalel ben Uri ben Chur of the tribe of Yehuda.' Let us imagine what that was like. Hashem assigned the task to Betzalel ben Uri. Now Moshe is going around asking people, 'Are you Betzalel ben Uri?' Again and again, the reply is, 'No, I'm Reuven ben Yaakov,' or 'No, I'm Shimon ben Yosef.'

"Does it make sense," Reb Elchanan continued, "that Moshe Rabbeinu would get angry at any of these people for not being Betzalel ben Uri? After all, what can they do? They weren't chosen by Hashem to build the *Mishkan*.

"What happened here is the same," Rav Elchanan concluded. "Where is there room for a grudge if your shul was not chosen to be one of the builders of Torah at this time, if you lack the merit to support the *Mishkan*?"

**There's giving**...and there's giving. There's giving so that you can feel like a big shot or have a plaque put up in your name, and there's giving to ease your conscience. Then, of course, there's also the real giving — giving purely for the sake of heaven, for the sake of the mitzva itself.

There is a story in the Gemara about Nachum Ish Gamzu (*Taanis* 21). A poor man once begged him for some food and he said, "Wait until I unload my donkey." Before Nachum Ish Gamzu had finished, though, the poor man died of starvation. Nachum Ish Gamzu was so repentant, he cried out, "My eyes that had no mercy should become blind! These hands that had no mercy should be cut off!" He went on in this way, and G-d heard his prayer. The heavenly decree came down, and Nachum Ish Gamzu became a paraplegic.

Reb Shlomo Zalman of Kelm once explained that although Nachum Ish Gamzu couldn't really be blamed for what had happened, he still did bear some responsibility. He should have been prepared for such circumstances, and should have had food ready to give right away — he shouldn't have needed to take care of something else first.

**Reb Tzvi Elimelech of Dinov** used to say: "Why don't we make a blessing before we give *tzedaka*, the way we make blessings on everything else? Because, had we been so commanded, the poor person could have very well starved to death by the time we finished making our blessing! If the *baal habayis* is a chassid, he would first have to go to the mikve, then he would have to recite a lengthy *leshem yichud*. By the time he got through all the preliminaries, the poor fellow would most probably have dropped dead!

**Rabbi Mendel of Riminov** was once visited by a poor man who cried bitterly about his situation. When he was done, Rabbi Mendel gave him a nice amount of money. After the man left, Rabbi Mendel called him back and gave him a few more coins.

The Riminover's relatives watched this with interest. They asked him what he had meant by calling the man back.

He said, "The first time I gave him money, I did it because I felt sorry for him. Giving him the money made me feel better. The second time, I gave him money for the sake of giving, not for my own sake."

**There is a similar story told** about Rabbi Simcha Bunim of Peshischa. He was once heading home from Danzig, and on the way he passed through a town where a certain Reb Zalman the Chassid lived. This Reb Zalman was famous for his profound Torah knowledge and kindness, as well as for being an extremely poor man. When Rabbi Simcha Bunim arrived at the town's inn, he sent for Reb Zalman right away.

It was bitter cold outside, and snowing heavily. When Reb Zalman arrived, he was wearing clothing shot through with holes, barely held together by patches. "Go," said Rabbi Simcha Bunim, "and prepare a complete meal for me." He gave Reb Zalman all the money he would possibly need for plentiful food and drink, and more.

After Reb Zalman left, Rabbi Simcha Bunim summoned the local furrier and bought a fur coat, a pair of high boots, and other items from him. Right before the meal was scheduled to begin, Rabbi Simcha Bunim told the innkeeper to bring all of the clothing to Reb Zalman's. Then, the rabbi himself headed over to Reb Zalman's home. He saw how poorly dressed and shod all of Reb Zalman's family was, and made sure that each and every member of the family was provided with the proper clothing.

They all sat down to eat. Afterward, when Rabbi Simcha Bunim was preparing to leave, Reb Zalman approached him to ask for a blessing. The rabbi handed him another gold coin.

"Rebbe," Reb Zalman protested, "I still have plenty of money left over from what you gave me for the food! And you've already given us all of this clothing!"

"How right you are, my friend," said Rabbi Simcha Bunim. "Before, I gave you the money and the clothing because I couldn't stand to see you going around in tatters. I gave you those things to ease my own conscience. Now, I want to give this to you purely for the sake of the mitzva."

**Rav Zerach Idelitz,** one of the outstanding Torah scholars of Prague, suffered a great financial loss in his old age and fell into debt. With a heavy heart, he came to discuss his problem with Rav Yechezkel Landau, the Rav of Prague.

At this time, the wedding of Rav Landau's daughter was approaching. Hidden in the rav's closet was the sum of three thousand gold pieces to be used for the wedding.

After hearing Rav Idelitz, Rav Landau asked, "How much would you need to pay your creditors and regain your previous standing?"

"Three thousand gold coins," responded Rav Idelitz.

Immediately, Rav Landau stood up, took the three thousand gold coins from the closet and gave them to Rav Idelitz.

Soon thereafter, Rav Landau's wife opened the closet and was shocked to find the money missing. Distraught, she came to tell her husband. He reassured her, saying he had loaned the money to a reliable individual.

She insisted that he reveal the borrower's identity to her. When he did, she cried out bitterly, "The whole city knows about Rav Idelitz's precarious financial situation. He is greatly in debt."

Rav Landau calmed his wife, assuring her that she had nothing to worry about, since Rav Idelitz was a G-d-fearing man who would surely pay on time.

As the wedding day drew closer, Rav Landau received a request that he offer his opinion in a *din Torah* held in the city of Fiorda concerning the estate of a wealthy man who had passed away.

Rav Landau sent back a responsum (which appears in *Noda Biyehuda*, 1st edition, *Choshen Mishpat* 30), which was accepted as the final ruling.

The two inheritors of the estate decided of their own accord to send Rav Landau *psak* gelt in the amount of three thousand gold coins. When the money arrived, Rav Landau turned to his wife and said, "Rav Idelitz's debt has been paid in full, down to the last penny."

**Once, when I was "down under"** in Australia raising money for the yeshiva, I heard the following story from a *baal habayis*. (Usually, I tell the stories, but this time...)

The fund-raiser of the Volozhin Yeshiva was about to set out on his yearly trip to raise money for the yeshiva. Before going, he asked to speak to the *rosh yeshiva*, Rav Chaim Soloveitchik.

"Every time I travel," the fund-raiser explained to the *rosh yeshiva*, "I have to hire a horse and carriage to get from place to place. My schedule is at the driver's mercy. Because of this, many times I am forced to rent a room in an inn for the night, losing time and money at the yeshiva's expense. Wouldn't it be better if the yeshiva bought its own horse and carriage to facilitate my travel?"

As the *rosh yeshiva* listened, the fund-raiser brought up another point. "Also, wouldn't I better represent the yeshiva if I dressed in a more presentable way? After all, most of the people I go to see are wealthy. My own clothes are almost threadbare."

Reb Chaim heard and agreed.

Several months later, the fund-raiser returned to the yeshiva with the donations he had collected. When Reb Chaim went over the lists, he was surprised to see that one of the yeshiva's regular supporters had not given a cent. He asked the fund-raiser why, but the latter could offer no explanation.

Since a significant amount was involved, Reb Chaim decided to visit the wealthy man himself.

"This year your representative drove up in a fancy carriage," the *baal habayis* said. "If the yeshiva can afford luxuries like that, it doesn't need my money. Not only will I never give you another ruble, but I also regret giving to the yeshiva in the past. I thought my money was going to Torah, not expensive suits for your fund-raiser and a fancy carriage to boot."

"Let me explain," said Reb Chaim. "Where the money goes depends on the donor's sincerity. If he gives because he wants to support Torah, that's where his money will go. Money given by someone whose motivation is less lofty will find its way to a less lofty expenditure. It all depends on you."

When the wealthy man heard that, he gave his regular yearly donation and continued to do so from then on.

**Poverty was the rule** in the Vilna Gaon's time, and
his household was no exception. Days could pass without his
family seeing a slice of bread. Once, his wife came to ask him
what to do about the hunger in their house. "What should I do
for the children? They're begging me for bread we don't
have!"

"Take them to the neighbors," her husband answered.
"When their children eat, they will feed our children, too."

When people found out about the family's situation, a hue
and cry arose. "There's a tzaddik among us, and his family has
nothing to eat!"

A very wealthy woman named Leah decided to support the
Gaon's family. She went to Reb Leibel, the son of one of the pillars of the community, to find out how much the Gaon needed
so that his family could live untroubled.

Reb Leibel thought about it and said, "Three gold pieces
every week is what they need to get by."

After the woman left, Reb Leibel got to thinking. "What a
mitzva, supporting the Gaon's family! I can't just pass this up."
He immediately dispatched a messenger with three gold pieces
to the Gaon's house.

A short time later, the wealthy woman's servant arrived at
the Gaon's home with the same amount of money. The Gaon
refused to accept it, since he had already been given what he
needed by Reb Leibel. When the rich woman heard about the
Gaon's refusal, she came to Reb Leibel to protest.

"This is what you do? I decide to do this mitzva, and you
steal it from me?"

"But, I couldn't stand by and not do the mitzva myself!"

She summoned him to the court of the *dayan* of Vilna, and
they both stated their claims.

The judge's decision was that each of them should give the Gaon three gold pieces a week.

**The rich face many tests** in giving. A good friend of mine who is known to be a big *baal chessed* shared this story with me.

He traveled to Eretz Yisrael for a friend's wedding together with his thirteen-year-old son. When he arrived at the airport, several people representing various charitable institutions came to meet him and lay out the red carpet. Anyone might have anticipated what would happen when they all converged on the traveler in the airport. Each began to fight for the privilege of taking the man and his son to Yerushalayim, and a real ruckus ensued. As such things often go, the end result was that one suitcase was left behind.

"That single suitcase held my best clothing," said my wealthy friend. "I had come for a wedding, and I had also planned to visit some of the tzaddikim, so I had packed my very best things: my good suits, my favorite cuff links, expensive shoes that were brand-new. What's worse, when I stopped in New York, I met a friend who took me shopping. This friend convinced me to buy some very expensive shirts, and the suitcase also contained some of my favorite (actually irreplaceable) ties. Not only that, but all of my son's best clothing and shoes were in the suitcase, too."

He had to spend the entire following day shopping with his son.

"I felt pretty bad about what happened," he continued, "but I really learned the meaning of the sages' advice about running away from honor. I have gone to Eretz Yisrael so many times, and I have never lost a single suitcase. Yet this time, when all these people came out to honor me (and I accepted the ride to Yerushalayim), I lost all of my most precious belongings!"

My friend then told me that he had really learned his lesson, and that it would be the last time he would accept any honor.

My heart went out to him for his loss, but it was impossible not to see the hand of Hashem at work.

**The Chofetz Chaim** had a disciple whose Torah learning and fear of heaven were formidable. But he was so poor, he made other poor people seem rich. He would say to his revered teacher, "If I were a rich man, I would give generously to every cause that came my way."

Whenever the Chofetz Chaim heard this, he would just shake his head.

Some time later, this student traveled to St. Petersburg, where he went into business and became wealthy in a short time. Once his star rose, however, he failed the test and became miserly. The wealthier he grew, the more tightly he held on to his money.

Once, the Chofetz Chaim traveled to St. Petersburg and stopped in to see his former student.

"I'm doing well," said the wealthy man, "sound in body and pocket."

"How is your charitableness doing?" the Chofetz Chaim asked.

His former student blanched.

"I'll tell you a story," said the Chofetz Chaim. "A simple villager once traveled to the city to buy staples. He came to the grocer and asked for flour. 'Go right ahead and take whatever you like,' said the grocer. 'Just put it on the scale.'

"The villager kept piling flour on the scale. As he did so, the shopkeeper added weights to the other side to counterbalance the flour. When the villager stopped putting flour on the scale, the grocer added up the weights to calculate the bill. It came to five rubles.

"'But I wanted only one ruble's worth of flour!' protested the villager.

"'Fool!' said the grocer. 'If you wanted only one ruble's

worth, why did you keep adding more flour onto the scale? Didn't you see that I kept adding weights to the other side so that I could tally up your bill?'

"This is your situation exactly," said the Chofetz Chaim. "A person keeps on running after money, piling it up, but he doesn't realize that the evil impulse is running right after him, weighing him down on the other side, compelling him not to give charity."

**The Chofetz Chaim** wrote (*Chomas Hadas* p. 39):

I am not surprised by the failure to support Torah study by the wealthy among the masses. I am surprised, though, by the affluent who, though scrupulous in their observance, neglect to support Torah study...

I know their excuses. Some think that since they give one ruble a year to a fund-raiser or some crumbs of bread to a *yeshiva bachur*, they have already fulfilled their mitzva of supporting Torah study. This is a mistake, because while this would be a sufficient donation for a poor man, for a rich man it is not.

One wealthy man told me that he gives to several yeshiva fund-raisers. He added up all his donations, and it came to a sum of twelve rubles a year. I pointed to one of the curtains in his living room and asked, "How much did that curtain cost?" He answered that it cost about twenty-five rubles.

"If so," I said, "then with six windows in the house, that adds up to 150 rubles!"

Such a thing should be a source of great embarrassment. He should give 150 rubles to support Torah study, which gives life to our soul in this world and the next. Instead, he thinks he has already fulfilled the mitzva of supporting Torah with what little he does give.

There are others who claim exemption from the obligation of supporting Torah, because they have many expenses, and their budget won't allow it. However, when you look into how such people manage their households, you find many unnecessary luxury items, for which there is always room in the budget.

**Rav Chaim Soloveitchik** once traveled to Minsk on behalf of the Volozhin Yeshiva to raise money to rescue the yeshiva from enormous debts. Two *gabbaim* of the yeshiva lived in Minsk, both of whom were outstanding Torah scholars, possessed of great piety and generosity.

When he arrived, Rav Chaim went to one of the two and explained to him the purpose of his visit. Despite the fact that the sum needed was very large, the *gabbai* assured Rav Chaim that he would take care of it, and Rav Chaim sat down to learn in the man's home.

After some time, Rav Chaim inquired as to whether the sum had been raised, and the *gabbai* responded that so far, half of the sum had been raised. Rav Chaim happily returned to his learning.

After a month had gone by, Rav Chaim inquired again as to the remaining half, and the *gabbai* responded that he now had the full amount needed. Rav Chaim returned to Volozhin and paid the yeshiva's debts.

A short time afterward, the two *gabbaim* arrived in Volozhin to have a *din Torah*. Infuriated, the second *gabbai* accused the *gabbai* Rav Chaim had visited of paying Rav Chaim the entire sum from his own pocket and not splitting the mitzva with him as they had always done in the past. The second *gabbai* demanded that he be able to contribute half of the sum.

When Rav Chaim realized that the *gabbai* who had hosted him had paid the full sum from his own pocket, he asked, "Why did you keep me in your home for an entire month? Why didn't you just give me the full amount right away?"

"Is it such an easy thing to just take such a large amount out of one's pocket?" asked the *gabbai*. "I had to work very hard to overcome the trait of greed to give the first half, and afterward, I had to keep struggling, waging an inner battle until I convinced myself to give the other half."

**The Volozhin Yeshiva was in dire straits,** with bills accumulating, and no money to pay them. Creditors came to the Netziv and told him they could no longer extend even a penny's worth of credit to the institution. It was then that the Netziv advised Rav Chaim Soloveitchik to travel to Minsk in search of support for the yeshiva.

Reb Chaim immediately set off on his mission and soon arrived in Minsk. Once there, he wasted no time is going to see one of the wealthiest Jews in town. He described the yeshiva's plight, but the rich man interrupted him. "Rabbi, go back to your inn and get a good night's sleep. We'll discuss the matter tomorrow."

Reb Chaim had no choice but to return to the inn, but he felt dispirited and worried about the yeshiva's future.

Early in the morning, the wealthy man came to Reb Chaim's inn with a companion.

"Rabbi, my uncle and I need you to decide a matter of halacha for us."

"I'm sorry," said Reb Chaim. "I'm not a judge, and I came to Minsk only to raise money for the yeshiva."

Nevertheless, the men stood their ground and insisted that Reb Chaim hear them out. He finally agreed to listen to their arguments.

The younger man began, "Rabbi, when you came to me last night, I decided then and there to give you thirty thousand rubles for the yeshiva. When my uncle heard about your cause, though, he said he also wanted to contribute. I told him he was nosing in on my territory. He claimed it wasn't a business deal, but a mitzva, and said he feels he has the right to give half the amount.

"Friends," said Reb Chaim, "The best person to answer your question is the Netziv himself. Go and speak to him."

The uncle and nephew traveled to Volozhin together. When the Netziv heard their case, he decided they were both in the right. He told the younger man to donate thirty thousand rubles, and the uncle to give fifteen thousand. And that saved the yeshiva.

**Once, a wealthy man** who had always given large sums of money to *tzedaka* suffered a financial setback and lost most of his money. He came to Rav Chaim of Volozhin to ask his advice.

"I'm not coming to ask about my own needs," he began. "My concern is the charity I usually give. To continue giving *tzedaka* as usual, I would have to borrow. According to halacha, should I decrease the amount of *tzedaka* I give, even though it would be hard for me to see the suffering of the poor people who depend on me? Or, should I borrow money to continue giving *tzedaka*, even though going into debt might ruin any future chances I have of getting back on my feet?"

Rav Chaim thought intently before giving his advice. Then he said, "Continue giving *tzedaka* as you used to, in line with the dictates of your compassionate heart. As for your financial situation, you are already promised by *Chazal* that 'one who comes to purify himself is given assistance.'"

Weeks went by, and then word arrived from the formerly wealthy man:

"I have just won half a million rubles in the lottery!"

Rav Chaim's joy was visible to all, as once again the promise of *aser bishvil shetisasher* (one should give a tenth of one's profits in order to become rich) had been fulfilled.

**Rav Yonasan Eibeshitz** married the daughter of a very wealthy man, and received a dowry of thirty thousand gold rubles. After the wedding, he continued to sit and learn Torah day and night in the *beis medrash* with his *chavrusa* just as he had before.

Out of spite, the gentiles built a church directly across the street from the study hall in such a way that anyone going into the *beis medrash* couldn't help but see the cross on the church's roof.

Rabbi Yonasan Eibeshitz's learning partner was so disturbed by this intrusion that he could stand it no longer. One dark night, he climbed onto the church's roof and broke the cross.

Unfortunately, he was caught in the act.

The next day, people noticed he was missing. They searched everywhere, but they couldn't find him; he had vanished. In the midst of the tumult, the gentile watchman came to a member of the Jewish community and told him what had happened. The Jew had been arrested, and was going to be burned at the stake for his crime!

This gentile watchman knew that the church had a back exit, and told community members that their fellow Jew could escape that way. The risk was great, and the watchman would agree to smuggle the Jew out of the church only for the astronomical sum of thirty thousand rubles, not one ruble less.

People were shocked by the terrible report and appalled at the sum of money being asked of them. However, the mitzva of *pidyon shevuyim*, redeeming captives, was precious to them. Moreover, it wasn't just about releasing someone from captivity; if they didn't succeed, he would be executed!

Pairs of collectors began their task, going from door to door throughout the Jewish streets.

Rav Yonasan Eibeshitz heard what was being done, but he alone realized the urgency of the situation. Waiting until all the money was accumulated from small donations might endanger the captive's life.

178 / It's How You Give

It wasn't long after his wedding, and Reb Yonasan still had the dowry money in his house. He ran home, took the thirty thousand rubles from its hiding place, and gave it to the Christian watchman immediately.

The watchman was true to his word and did, indeed, help the Jew escape from the church and flee to another city.

Reb Yonasan returned to the *beis medrash.*

Meanwhile, the community's collectors scraped together as much as they could and headed over to Reb Yonasan to give the money to him. When they arrived, he calmly told them that he had already given the watchman the entire sum, and that there was no longer any need for their money.

"You raised the money, it's true," they said to him, "but still, we collected this money for that purpose. Even though we couldn't come up with the entire thirty thousand, everyone gave as much as he could. We also want a part of the mitzva."

"I'm sorry," said Reb Yonasan, "but the money has already been paid. The effort you put into collecting the money will bring you all a share in the mitzva."

On the way home, Reb Yonasan began to worry. "What will happen when my wife finds out? She'll be furious. We're not talking about a small sum of money!" He decided to leave town for a few days. He figured that in his absence, she would assume they had been robbed. Hopefully, by the time he returned, she would have gotten over the shock.

In the meantime, on the other side of town, the gentiles discovered that the Jew had escaped, and they correctly deduced that the watchman had been his accomplice. They decided to do to the watchman what they had planned to do to the Jew. Who knew? The watchman might even be Jewish himself!

When the watchman got wind of their plans, he realized it was time to flee. He had been working for the government for forty years, and during that time had amassed a huge fortune of embezzled government money and goods. What could he do now? He couldn't exactly carry it all with him when he was on the run! He decided to take all of his money (along with his newly acquired thirty thousand rubles) and go over to Reb Yonasan's house.

Struggling to maintain his composure, he asked the rebbetzin where the rabbi was. She said he had gone out. Unable to control his trembling (time was running out), he told the entire story to the rebbetzin. He had to run, but he wasn't willing to leave his fortune to his murderers. He would rather leave it with Reb Yonasan, who had been willing to sacrifice all he had for the sake of another Jew. Whether he lived or died, he wanted a straight and true man like Reb Yonasan to have it. If he lived, then he knew he would get his money back when he returned for it. And if he died, then Reb Yonasan would surely do good things with his money.

The watchman ran for his life, but his fellow townspeople pursued him relentlessly. Eventually, they caught up with him and drowned him in the river.

Reb Yonasan's wife now knew the entire story. She knew that G-d had sent them all this wealth for all the good deeds her husband did. Not only did they get their own dowry money back, but they were showered with even more! She was thrilled.

Reb Yonasan, who was heading home, didn't know a thing about what had happened. As he approached the house, he was still trying to formulate a plan for breaking the news to his wife.

She saw him, and came out to greet him. "I already know everything that happened!" She then went on to tell him the rest of the story, believing that he would be just as happy as she was at their great good fortune. As she finished her story, however, Reb Yonasan began to cry bitterly, like a young child. Shocked, she asked him why he was so upset.

"I'm crying for the same reason you're happy," he answered. "The reward for a mitzva comes in the next world, not in this world. If I was rewarded here, then the mitzva I did is being thrown back in my face."

He resolved to fast for three consecutive days and then ask a *she'eilas chalom* (a mystical procedure where one can receive information from the next world). He asked why his mitzva had been rejected. The response he received was: "Yes, you did a great mitzva, but you didn't want to share it with the community. Go and take your reward."

**Many years ago in Italy** there lived a very wealthy businessman. Guests from out of town were always welcome in his luxurious home, but fund-raisers were treated royally. Their host was always first to give, and he gave very generously. He would also encourage his rich friends and others in the community to do the same. And if for some reason a person was unable to give his standard donation, either because he had run into hard times financially or because he was out of town, the *gevir* would himself give the fund-raiser the missing amount.

Like others of his social standing, this *gevir* had a personal attendant. This Yitzchak was very devoted to his master and eager to fulfill his every wish. He was also very naive. Everyone was amused by Yitzchak, but Yitzchak didn't realize it because of his naivete, and this went on for years.

Once, a famous rabbi came to town to raise funds. Naturally, he was hosted by the wealthy man in his home. After spending several weeks in town collecting money, the time for him to leave drew near.

The day before the rabbi left, the wealthy man called his servant to him and said, "Yitzchak, the rabbi who is staying with us is raising money for people learning in Eretz Yisrael. He is ready to return home, but he doesn't want to leave without your donation."

Yitzchak accepted this statement at face value, and immediately left the room, only to return a few minutes later with a small pouch filled with coins.

"This is all I have," the servant said. "Even though it's not much, I'd be happy if the rav would accept this so that I, too, can have a share in this wonderful mitzva."

The fund-raiser, who had watched the whole scene, didn't know what to do. Should he accept the money or not? After all, it was all the money Yitzchak had.

Just then, Yitzchak's master said to him, "Empty your pockets of all your money, and the rav will give you a blessing befitting your deed."

Yitzchak did this and went to get a blessing.

The rav was struck by Yitzchak's sincerity and, with tears in his eyes, gave Yitzchak a blessing that he would become as honored and as wealthy as all the other *gevirim*. "When I come again, may you be able to give me just as much as your master." Then he kissed the boy's hands and took his leave.

The town where Yitzchak and his master lived was a seaport where ships from all over the world came to dock. Most of their merchandise consisted of goods stolen by the many pirates that used to roam the seas. They would bring their booty to auction in that town.

One day, when the auction was taking place, Yitzchak happened to find himself among the crowd at the docks. He stood there watching in fascination.

After a while, he grew tired from standing so long in one spot, and casually rested a hand on a nearby wooden crate and shifted his weight. Little did he know that in so doing, he was placing a bid.

The custom in the town was that would-be buyers did not call out their bids. Instead, all they had to do was set their hand on a crate, and the auctioneer would take it as a sign that they wanted to raise the bid.

When the auctioneer saw Yitzchak place his hand on the crate, he quite naturally thought that Yitzchak was there to represent his master. Since Yitzchak kept his hand on the box, his was the highest bid, and the container was sold to Yitzchak's master.

That afternoon, just as the *gevir* was about to leave, he saw wagon after wagon pulling up to his house.

"What's this all about?" he asked the workers.

In reply, they thrust a bill of lading into his hand. On it was a list of all he had bought at such a place and at such a price through his servant, Yitzchak.

The master called Yitzchak over to find out what happened. Eventually, he was able to piece together what had really taken place.

He realized that Yitzchak hadn't done anything intentionally wrong. Still, he was now stuck with all the crates. He ordered a servant to open several of them. To his disappointment, they all contained bolts of fabric. This was not his line of business. His best option would be to get rid of the goods as quickly as possible.

He was so irritated by the incident that he ordered the crates put into storage, and dismissed the whole incident from his mind.

Several weeks later, he decided to get rid of the crates. He opened the boxes to get a better look at the merchandise so he would know what kind of a deal to make. To his surprise, he found that the crates didn't contain material as was written on the bill of lading, but money. The top layer inside each box was a bolt of fabric that hid beneath it gold, silver and currency from all over the world.

After a few moments of thought, he realized that the treasure before his eyes must be a fulfillment of the visiting rav's blessing.

That night, when the *gevir* went to bed, he tossed and turned, trying to decide who the money should go to. Should it go to his loyal servant, Yitzchak? After all, the rav's blessing was given to him. On the other hand, the bill of lading was made out in his own name.

He fell asleep after hours of thought and dreamed that the rav came on his yearly visit to raise money. "I heard you became wealthy," the rav said to Yitzchak. "Why isn't your name on the list with all the other donors?"

Before the rav could finish speaking, the *gevir* woke up and fainted.

Later that day, he called Yitzchak over and showed him the contents of the boxes and said he had decided to give it all to him, except for the expenses he had incurred from the delivery. He told his servant that he saw this sudden wealth as fulfillment of the rav's blessing, and he told him about his dream.

Yitzchak thought the *gevir* was joking, since he was prone to such jokes, but when he saw that the *gevir* was serious, he believed completely that his good fortune was due to the rav's blessing.

They decided to open all the other boxes and found that they, too, were filled with gold and silver.

Yitzchak was able to go into business for himself and became as wealthy as all of the other *gevirim*. He decided that he wanted to use most of his time for learning, and that is exactly what he did. Eventually, he put down on paper all of his *chiddushim* (Torah thoughts). In his later years, he compiled and edited these notes, and printed them as a book, *Baal Sadeh Yitzchak* by Rabbi Yitzchak Itta.

# Americana

A friend of mine in the Midwest went collecting in his community for a worthy cause. Some people gave him their donation on the spot, while others told him they would give later.

Several weeks later, on Purim, he went to shul wearing a ten-gallon hat. Before and after the megilla reading, he made his way among the crowd to reach the people who had promised to give.

At the same time, there was a fund-raiser there who wasn't having it so easy. He noticed that no matter who the cowboy went over to, that person always gave him a check.

Finally, he went over to the successful fund-raiser and asked if he could borrow the ten gallon hat.

# Americana

Once, I was standing at the door of a potential donor's house with my hand poised to knock when I saw the *baal habayis* pull into the driveway. Now, when a person has just come home at the end of his day, you never know whether or not you've picked a good time to call on him. After a long day at the office, the *baal habayis* usually just wants to wash up and have supper. He may have other meetings to attend, or he may just want to unwind. Either way, he's got things to do. He'll either give you a check on the spot to get you on your way, or he'll ask you to come back later. That's why, when this *baal habayis* pulled up, I knew I had to come up with a good line fast.

Before he even had a chance to acknowledge me, I smiled

confidently and said, "*Yashar ko'ach*. Thank you. I really appreciate that you came home now just in time to meet me. Thank you for saving me another trip out here." With this joke, I hoped to create the right atmosphere for a quick donation. Since I only have so much time at my disposal for making my rounds, I prefer to get my check and be on my way to the next stop.

"Sorry," the *baal habayis* answered, also smiling, "but you've got it wrong. I knew you were here. I saw you from a few blocks away."

I was dumbfounded. "From a few blocks away?" I stammered. "How's that?"

The *baal habayis* explained that recent technological innovations make it possible for him to keep an eye on his property via a closed-circuit camera whose screen is in his car! With crime on the rise, he wanted the added safety such a system offers. This way, if a mugger tried to hide in the bushes that line his walkway, he'd know about it before he got home.

**There was once** a young man who grew up in Boro Park, the "capital" of Diaspora *frumkeit*, in a family that was adamant about their affiliation with Reform. They even balked at their son's eating in a kosher restaurant — in a neighborhood where almost all of the restaurants were kosher anyway! This young man joined the U.S. Army and eventually joined the division called the U.S. Rangers, the roughest and toughest division of the army. These are the fellows who jump from planes, who go into battle alongside the marines.

This young man was stationed in southern Georgia. His parents must have thought that being in the army, with the Rangers in southern Georgia, their son would definitely be safe from the influence of any Orthodox rabbis. Little did they realize that he was stationed in Savannah, which at that time had the only army base in America within walking distance of a large Orthodox shul with a well-established *kollel*. It took a mere six months for Rabbi Slatus and the head of the *kollel*, Rabbi

Burstein, to help this young man along the path of growth in *Yiddishkeit*.

When the prodigal son returned to Boro Park, the rabbi down South received a telephone call from an irate mother.

"Why didn't you just mind your own business?" she fumed. "Now my own son won't eat in my house!"

The young man eventually went on to study in a local yeshiva, became *shomer Shabbos*, and married and raised a fully observant family. And all of this started with a flight from Judaism!

**In a southeastern U.S. community,** there is a fast-food restaurant that serves the area. One of the waitresses there is a *baalas teshuva*, but not too many people know why she is so willing to accept every new mitzva she learns about so quickly.

The waitress is a Russian immigrant who used to be an Olympic-class diver. She was just beginning to accept a Torah life when she found out that she would have to fly on Shabbos to participate in the Olympics. She asked her rabbi what to do. Obviously, he told her that traveling on Shabbos is absolutely forbidden.

When she went to tell her manager that she wouldn't be able to travel on Shabbos, he said, "You're making a grave mistake. You barely speak English, and you won't be able to get another job so easily. Even if you do, it will never compare with the one you have now, since you're making a fantastic salary, and you get so many fringe benefits! If you really won't travel on Saturday, I'll have to let you go."

The Olympian diver ran back to her rabbi crying that she didn't know what to do. He told her, "Put your trust in G-d, and you'll see for yourself that you didn't make a mistake."

She took the leap and put her trust in G-d. Within days, she realized she had made the right decision. Had she been on the Atlanta-bound ValuJet flight her manager booked her for, she would have gone down over the Florida Everglades on May 11,

1996 with the rest of the passengers, none of whom survived.

**People's memories** and *neshamos* are often stirred by things that don't seem all that significant.

One of the donors to my yeshiva once told me that when she was a little girl in Europe, her father always sat at the back of the shul. This was surprising, since he was considered one of the more prominent members of the community. Whenever anyone asked why he sat at the back, he would answer that he always wanted to catch all of the fund-raisers and people who had nowhere to eat so that he could bring them home with him. He would then send his daughter ahead to tell his wife to prepare the extra place settings for their unexpected guests. After some time, his wife got used to his way of doing things, and would always prepare additional place settings every week.

One Pesach, this *baal habayis* brought home an additional ten or eleven guests. As he handed out the Haggadas, one of the guests began to cry uncontrollably. The *baal habayis* asked him what was wrong, and the man answered, "This is the exact same Haggada that I sold to you ten years ago. At that time, I was irreligious, and I needed money. I sold a whole bunch of books, and you bought them, since you were afraid that otherwise they would be thrown in the garbage, G-d forbid. Now here it is back in my hands!"

**Gene had become observant,** but his older brother Mark was still estranged from traditional Judaism. But let's start at the very beginning. When Mark was born, his mother and father had been vehemently opposed to circumcising their newborn son. After a short time, their "intact" baby developed an infection at the site where there should have been a circumcision. Even so, they didn't feel that his lack of a bris was to blame for the infection. When their second son, Gene, was born, however, they decided to play it safe and circumcise him.

Isn't it interesting how things turned out? The brother who had no bris never made a commitment to *Yiddishkeit*, and the brother who was circumcised did!

**Mrs. Yager observed Shabbos** and the holidays, and always lit candles. As her family grew, and the children had children of their own, the youngsters drifted away from *Yiddishkeit*. Many years down the line, after two generations of assimilation, her great-grandson found his way back to an observant life. He married a girl who had also found her way to traditional Jewish observance several years earlier. They were the only *shomrei Shabbos* members of each of their respective family lines.

After seven years of marriage, they were finally blessed with a daughter. The new mother felt an affinity for the name Rivka, and so their baby girl was given that name instead of the name of a departed family member, as is customary.

Now, Mrs. Yager, the husband's great-grandmother who had been observant, had left her Shabbos candlesticks to her daughter, her only living relative. This daughter had unfortunately never used them, but when she heard that her grandson was a religious Jew and was married, she sent him these candlesticks. Years later, when the grandmother passed away, none of the members of the family were on hand. A neighbor came in to the grandmother's house and walked off with every valuable in her home. So it turned out that the only items of value that remained within the family circle were these candlesticks that the grandmother had sent to her grandson before she passed on.

Several years later, to their surprise, the couple discovered that the great-grandmother's Jewish name had been Rivka.

**After much spiritual searching,** a young man finally decided that he wanted to become a Jew. He spoke with a rabbi several times and was then told to go see a different rabbi in New York. Many learning sessions later, the rabbi in New York saw that the young man was still serious about conversion. He asked the young man, "Are you doing this because you have a Jewish girlfriend?"

When the young man said no, the rabbi asked him a few more pertinent questions. Ultimately, the rabbi converted this young man.

Several months later, the young man was walking down the street when he bumped into an old acquaintance. They traded small talk for a few minutes, after which the acquaintance asked how the young man's family was doing back home. He answered that he had broken off all contact with his family since he had converted to Judaism.

The other person looked at him as if he had fallen off the moon. "What do you mean you converted? Your mother was Jewish!"

**A fund-raiser should never think** that since he's on the road and has a certain route, he eventually becomes part of the scenery. After going to a certain city for over ten years, I once arrived a week later than usual. When I came to the house where I normally stayed, the woman immediately asked if everything was all right.

"You always come during the exact same week, every year like clockwork. I couldn't figure out what on earth could have happened to you! I wanted to call your wife. The only reason I didn't call Eretz Yisrael was because I didn't want to worry her."

She had just decided to put off the call for another few days when I strolled in.

**A friend of mine** once went to daven with an early minyan in New York. As is customary, the *gabbai* honored the guest with *shishi*. In that particular shul, during the sixth aliya, they say the prayer for all those who are ill. At this time, people in the congregation approach the *bima* with names. One person comes with one name, another comes with two, and so forth.

One man, however, approached the *gabbai* with over thirty names. Several names is understandable, but thirty names is unusual, to say the least. You would have thought a major epidemic had broken out. Even stranger was that all the names were clearly of people from different families, since none of the mothers had the same name. To top it all off, the man rattled off all the names by heart. He had no list, nothing. It was unbelievable.

As my friend made his way back to his seat, one of the regulars told him the story. "That man with the thirty names is a doctor. He has a photographic memory, and every Shabbos, he comes over to the *gabbai* and tells him the names of all his Jewish patients."

**Irving M. Bunim** had a reputation as a philanthropist and a fund-raiser among his circle of acquaintances. He once decided to hold a social evening for his friends. When very few of them showed up, Mr. Bunim made inquiries as to why not many of the guests had bothered to come. Their replies all amounted to the same sentiment: "You didn't have to make a social evening. Just call us up, and we'll make our pledges over the phone!"

**In certain cities,** I find that I am more successful when I make the rounds together with a member of the local community. In one case, I took the rabbi along with me. When we got to the door of a certain *baal habayis*, the man's wife answered our knock and invited us in. When we asked to see her husband, she said, "Today is Sunday, so he's at work."

In America, most people take Sunday off like everyone else, so we were a little confused. The wife picked up on our confusion and said, "Doesn't the Torah say: Six days shall you work, and rest on the Shabbos?"

Now that's a real *baal habayis*!

**I'll never forget the time** my knock at the door of a *baal habayis* was answered by a child who said, "Please come and sit in the den. But take off your shoes first."

The reason was obvious — they didn't want scuff marks on their parquet floors. Needless to say, it was a humbling experience. I consider myself lucky I didn't have holes in my socks that day.

**In my travels,** I've met people with all kinds of interesting customs. I was once staying in a city where the closest shul was an hour's walk from my hosts' home. On Friday, everyone drives to shul and naturally walks home after davening. The first time I stayed in the city, I saw that after we had all walked home Friday night, everyone sat down on the sofas and easy chairs and began to sing "Shalom Aleichem." Now, every other family sings "Shalom Aleichem" at the table, so I asked why they did it sitting on the couches.

My host answered, "It was my father's custom."

I asked, "But where did your father get the custom from?"

He said, "Well, since it was such a long walk home from shul, everyone would always collapse into the closest chair Friday night and sing "Shalom Aleichem" sitting down, just to catch their breath."

**When Mrs. K. was a little girl,** a fund-raiser would come to her parents' house every year to collect money. As her parents wrote out their check, she would run to her room and scrape together some of the money she had saved from her weekly allowance of twenty-five cents. True, the fifteen cents she donated wasn't much, but she would always receive her very own official receipt in the mail a few weeks later. It must have cost at least that much to print the thing, but she was thrilled to receive it.

The next year, she raised the amount of her donation from fifteen cents to a full twenty-five. Yet again, she received an official receipt from the institution. This fund-raiser was a real mensch — every donation was acknowledged, no matter how small. Who knows, maybe even then he knew he was sowing seeds that would blossom later on into Mrs. K.'s famous hospitality and generosity.

**Great people realize** that those seeds can be sown. Rav Moshe Feinstein once came to a city and stayed at the home of a certain *baal habayis*. Whenever Rav Moshe stayed there, the *baal habayis* would have his son sleep in another room to afford their illustrious visitor the hospitality he deserved of a private room.

Eventually, Rav Moshe found out that the boy had been displaced to furnish him with his room every year. He made sure to stop off at the boy's yeshiva before heading back to New York to give him a *yashar ko'ach* for being so generous.

**One of the most outstanding stories** of my entire tenure as a fund-raiser took place when I went to visit a doctor's home, accompanied by one of the local rabbis in a certain town.

We knocked at the door and a youngster asked, "Who is it?"

"It's Rabbi So-and-so," I answered.

The boy opened the door for us and invited us in. He asked if we were hungry or thirsty.

"No, thanks," we both murmured politely. "We're fine."

We took seats, and asked if his father was home.

The youngster said, "No, he isn't here right now. Could you

tell me something about your mission?"

"We're here to collect funds for a yeshiva in Eretz Yisrael. Is your mother at home?"

"My mother isn't here right now, either. What is the name of the yeshiva? Are donations to the yeshiva tax deductible? Do you have a brochure that I could look at, and have you ever been to our home before?"

Despite our surprise at these types of questions coming from someone his age, we provided him with the information he asked for. He took a few minutes to digest it, and then excused himself, asking us to wait for him where we were.

"I'll be back in just a minute," he said.

A few moments later, the youth returned with a large check-book, and asked, "Do I make the check out the same way that the yeshiva's name appears on the brochure?"

We answered in the affirmative, and he proceeded to write out a check. He handed it to me, we thanked him, and he began to see us to the front door. Before we left, I asked him three questions that I'm sure would have been on anyone's mind.

"How old are you, if you don't mind my asking?"

"I'm sixteen," he answered.

"I hope you won't be offended, but how is it that a sixteen-year-old is writing checks like this?"

The boy explained that his father was a doctor who lectured all over the country. He was often away from home, and so was his mother. His parents had told him that if a rabbi ever came to the door, he should invite him in and offer him something to eat and drink. Then he should make sure to give the rabbi a check so that he didn't have to come back and waste his valuable time.

I then asked, "What yeshiva do you attend?"

"Oh, I don't go to yeshiva. I go to public school."

We thanked him again, and took our leave.

As soon as we got into the car, I started it right away and asked the rabbi who was with me to please refrain from saying anything. I pulled away from the curb, drove for a few blocks, and then parked the car. I turned to the rabbi and asked him what he was thinking.

We both agreed that this was no run-of-the-mill kind of situation. Neither of us had ever heard of anything like it. We both felt a strong desire to do whatever we could to get the boy into some sort of a yeshiva. However, this was never translated into action.

The next year, the sister answered the door and asked us to sit in the den while she summoned her brother. He came, asked us the same questions as he had the previous year, and gave us another check — this time, for slightly more.

During my third visit to the house, I was privileged to meet the parents. I told them what had happened during the previous two years, and asked them the question that had been plaguing me (and the other rabbi) for the last two years.

"Why isn't he in yeshiva?"

The mother explained, "He used to learn in the local yeshiva, but he was very unhappy there. He wanted to switch to public school, but was willing to make the switch only if he would find two or three rabbis with whom he would commit to learn on a regular basis."

Smiling, she then said, "He isn't home right now, because he is learning in Eretz Yisrael this year."

**A friend of mine** once flew with a partner from the West Coast to the East Coast to raise money for their institution. Bear in mind that coming in from Eretz Yisrael to raise money in the States is difficult in its own right. Going from one city to another in the States is much, much more so. Generally, such fundraisers are not the first in line. They can't claim to be from Eretz

Yisrael, and the local institutions are usually beset by their own financial problems.

When my friend and his partner arrived at the home of a certain *baal habayis*, the man started railing at them, "Why bother wasting money flying from coast to coast?" And so on.

As fate would have it, there was a guest in the house who overheard his host. He tried to intervene and calm the man down, and as he did, he wrote out a check for the visitors so they could walk away with something more than just their own humiliation.

The very next year, the two fund-raisers headed back to the same city. By mistake, they knocked on the same man's door. When he opened the door, they didn't know what to do with themselves. Should they just walk off, or try again?

Before they could make a move, the *baal habayis* said, "Thank G-d you came back! I thought you would never show up at my door again after I embarrassed you that way last year. After you left, I felt so terrible about what I had done. Please come in. Can I make you a cup of coffee or something?"

As he puttered around his kitchen, the man went on. "The reason I'm so happy to see you is that I have been feeling just awful about it all year long. I've been hoping you'd come back, not only so that I can give you a check, which I'll do anyway, but because I want to ask your forgiveness."

That's not the end of the story, either. The following year when they returned, he hosted them in his home for two weeks!

**When I was on the West Coast** several years ago, I was staying at the house of a friend I had known for over twenty years. I had just flown in from the Midwest and, understandably, I was exhausted. When I came over to his house, he told me that I could stay with him, but that he and his wife might not be home, and the same went for the kids.

"My wife is due any minute," he explained. "If you want,

I can find you somewhere else to stay."

I was too tired to think about going anywhere else, so I stayed.

As things worked out, I ended up babysitting for them that night when they went to the hospital. I guess that was the first time in history that someone flew a couple of thousand miles to a friend's house to babysit for him.

# Inside Information

Mr. Black asked his friend, Mr. Green, who had recently gone on vacation, if the people in his resort town were friendly.

"As soon as I arrived," replied Mr. Green, "ten people ran over to welcome me."

"That's nice," murmured Mr. Black.

"The only problem is," continued Mr. Green, "eight of them were fund-raisers."

# Inside Information

**M**aking money for an institution means learning how to hustle. That means keeping on top of who is new in town, who just moved in and who just got married. People often ask me how I found them. In all my years as a fund-raiser, I've learned that the best answer is, "A few people mentioned your name since they are familiar with my institution and think so highly of it. They thought you would probably want to support such a worthy cause, too."

I still find that the best "new recruits" are the newlyweds. They don't have many financial obligations, like tuition or shul dues, and they really want to start off their marriage with as many mitzvos as possible. One of these mitzvos is giving *maaser*.

Just knowing who to call on, though, isn't nearly enough. No matter what position or stage of life you are in, one of the most important things to focus on when speaking to others is your delivery. This is even more important when you are trying to sell a product, and it is obviously crucial when you are representing an organization. There is a good chance that a large percentage of the people you meet have never heard of your institution, and a fair percentage of them would feel none the worse for never hearing of it at all. As long as you're tax deductible, you're just another write-off.

To convince people to part with their hard-earned money is a challenge, and to get them to give big money is even more of a challenge. That's why you have to work on your delivery. Think of all the good points of your institution. There may be a few, there may be many. Then reduce all of these good points to the size of a nutshell and come up with a spiel that takes no longer than two minutes to recite.

**Just recently, I met a man** who was running to a bar mitzva. I tried to talk to him, but he said he had no time, because he wanted to make it to the hall next door in time for the speech. When I told him I needed only two minutes, he heard me out and quickly ran to his car for his checkbook so he could make out a check to the yeshiva. He wished me success and ran off to his affair. I was out of there in two minutes flat and was able to continue on my rounds. He got his mitzva and didn't have to entertain me.

People aren't interested in long, drawn-out appeals. Get right to the point, and your donors will be happy with you.

**Speaking of keeping** your donors happy, never, and I do mean never, try to put a price tag on the mitzva by pressing a *baal habayis* for more money than what he's already offered you. You may very well walk away with a bigger check this year, but I can guarantee that you'll find it very difficult to find the *baal habayis* again the following year.

A lot of *baalebatim* will ask how much you think they should give. Never fall into the trap of setting an amount. The *baalebatim* who ask you this question are testing you. They want to see how high you'll go, how high your expectations are — and how big a fool you can make of yourself. When a *baal habayis* asks me this, I give the answer of the Shaarei Tzion: "You should give whatever amount you would like to receive if the shoe was on the other foot, and you were doing the collecting. Of course," I go on with a smile, "that's impossible. But do the best you can anyway."

If that response doesn't please the *baal habayis*, then just say that he should make out the check in some multiple of *chai*, which means "life" and has the numerical equivalent of eighteen. If you give any other answer, you'll only be putting your foot in your mouth and opening yourself up to all kinds of problems.

**To be successful,** a fund-raiser needs to be able to "read" people to some extent. Fund-raising is a job that demands good interpersonal skills, and a fund-raiser who hasn't got them can make some real blunders.

Your first encounter with a *baal habayis* usually will not net you a large donation. If the two of you hit it off well, though, the *baal habayis* will often decide to increase his donation as time goes on without being asked.

It pays to hone your ability to speak with people about the topics that interest them. If you have a donor who smokes a pipe, you might talk about the kind of tobacco he smokes, what he thinks makes a good blend, and why. It may take a few extra minutes of your time, but you'll soon see how much pleasure people take in talking about themselves, their habits and those things that appeal to them.

On one occasion, I asked a *mashgiach* about a product and sat through an entire discourse about it: the way it is supervised, what to watch out for, how it is shipped, and so on. You can be sure the conversation ultimately worked to the advantage of the yeshiva I represent. As a fringe benefit, I actually picked up quite a bit of knowledge about the topic. It never hurts to learn something new, and you never know when that knowledge will come in handy later on when you're speaking with another *baal habayis*.

My general rule is: Let the *baal habayis* do the talking. People like to lead the conversation, and the less you talk, the more the *baal habayis* will think you know. Whether this is true or not is irrelevant. The main thing is that the *baal habayis* thinks so. Besides, you won't learn much by doing the talking. You already know what you know. Let the *baal habayis* do the talking, and you'll be the wiser for it.

Naturally, every fund-raiser has his own particular approach and way of doing things. Some fund-raisers like to fly from one city to the other, see the wealthy *baalebatim*, and keep moving. This may work for them, but I prefer to leave a city only when I know I've completely finished it, which means that I've stopped at every place possible.

Now, don't think I like to hang around; on the contrary, I try to move on as quickly as I can. And working this way does mean that I wind up staying in places much longer than I would like. Yet my method has its advantages. If I see a fund-raiser working in one neighborhood, I just pick myself up and drive over to another one. I find that the *baalebatim* get restless when too many fund-raisers knock on their doors one after the other. They also dislike the fact that on Sunday, their only day home from work and the one day of the week they can spend with the family, people are forever knocking on their doors.

**There was the time,** though, many years ago, that I arrived at someone's home only to be told to wait my turn because there was another fund-raiser there ahead of me. Since I was sitting in the same room as the fund-raiser and the *baal* *habayis,* I couldn't help but overhear their conversation.

"What can I do for you?" the *baal habayis* asked.

"The last time I was here," answered the fund-raiser, "you gave me eighteen dollars. Do you think you could give me two times *chai* (thirty-six dollars) this year?"

I made some rapid calculations, and came up with an idea. I didn't know whether or not the other guy got what he asked for, but I did know that there are *baalebatim* who really don't like to have a price put before them. I've sometimes met *baalebatim* who have told me that had the fund-raiser not set an amount, he would have gotten much more. So I knew I was taking a chance, but since it was my first time meeting this *baal habayis,* I decided to try my luck.

After the first fund-raiser left, the *baal habayis* asked what he could do for me. I said, "The other fund-raiser asked for two times *chai.* Me, I'm a nice guy. I'm only asking for one times *chessed"*(seventy-two dollars). I didn't get the *chessed,* but I did get the two times *chai.*

I walked out of there feeling good for several reasons. First of all, I'd never met this man before. Second of all, this was a street where fund-raisers were constantly knocking on the doors. One woman from that neighborhood told me that though she handed out only five or ten dollar bills, she had managed to give away between five and ten thousand dollars in a single year! Third, even eighteen dollars was considered a very nice donation twenty years ago.

In my years as a fund-raiser, I've found that there are four types of potential donors: those who will see you only at the office, because they don't want their family life to be constantly disturbed; those who will see you only at home, because they want to be able to get their work done without interruption; those who don't mind being inconvenienced wherever they are for the sake of a mitzva; and those who never want to be bothered with fund-raisers.

**A few words about fund-raisers** from a man who ran a guesthouse for visitors in an American city:

"A fund-raiser is a man with a mission — it doesn't matter if the mission is his own, or the need of some institution. The more accomplished fund-raisers are the ones that possess what I consider the two keys to fund-raising success: *derech eretz* and the ability to organize. They have either spent considerable time in the States and know the territory, or they were trained as to how to go about their business effectively.

"Others, unfortunately, lack both of these prerequisites for success. They arrive on the scene, and they are already in a crisis. They may know only a few words of English, and so find themselves unable to get by, or they have no driver, because they didn't know how to arrange for one beforehand. With some, their interpersonal skills are none too polished.

"Such people don't make too much money on the whole. Had they done their homework before coming to the States, more often than not they would have found that it really doesn't pay to travel that distance, with all the headaches and expenses, just to make their twelve hundred or even five thousand dollars.

"Of course, there are always exceptions. But over the years, I spoke a great deal with our guests. I heard about their situations, and since I cashed many a check for them, I saw just what they were bringing in for all their work. People like that, those lacking either *derech eretz* or organization (or both), didn't make a lot of money at all.

"I have also encountered fund-raisers with sterling *middos*. Once, a European gentleman wound up fund-raising in the States. Like others, he didn't have much money to throw around, so he would travel by Greyhound bus rather than fly from city to city. In this case, the gentleman came into town quite early in the morning and then made his way over to our house. I got up early for shul, and when I opened the front door to leave at six o'clock, I found him standing there. He'd been waiting there patiently since four o'clock, quietly reciting

*Tehillim* the entire time on my doorstep. He didn't ring the bell or knock, because he couldn't bring himself to disturb us. He didn't want to wake the household.

"Another fund-raiser has become like a *zeidy* 18to our family. An old *talmid chacham*, whenever he is in New York, he calls to let me know he is on the way, and I pick him up at the bus terminal. He first came right after the birth of my daughter, and when she cried in the night, he would pick her up to rock her so that our rest wouldn't be disturbed.

"He was from Poland. He told me that once he went to pray on Yom Kippur in Moscow. The *baal tefilla* asked him whether or not he liked the place, and he answered that he didn't like it at all. Right after Yom Kippur, the KGB whisked him off to Siberia — for bad-mouthing the holy city of Moscow."

**A book on fund-raising** wouldn't be complete without a few of the classic jokes about this line of work.

### JOKE #1

On a flight to New York, the captain came over the PA system saying, "We seem to be having a problem, and we're going to have to make an emergency landing."

He then went on to explain the emergency procedures and, as an afterthought, said, "Praying is definitely in order. If there are any rabbis on board, they should please do something religious now."

At that, one rabbi stood up and made a heartfelt appeal.

### JOKE #2

There was a boy who once swallowed a coin and it became lodged in the boy's throat. The mother promptly sent the child with his big sister to Yankel the fund-raiser. When the fund-raiser asked why they came to him, the big sister said, "Because my mother said that you can get anything out of anyone."

### JOKE #3

Two people were shipwrecked and stranded on an island. One was busy preparing for Shabbos and taking care of all the other necessities to make the island habitable. The other did nothing whatsoever.

"How can you sit there, totally relaxed, given our precarious situation?" the first man asked the second.

"It's like this," said the second man. "I'm a regular contributor to my yeshiva. No matter where I went, they always found me. Their annual fund-raising dinner will be taking place in another few weeks. According to my calculations, they should be here shortly."

# Buyer Beware

A man came to beg for charity in a certain city where Rav Yisrael Salanter was staying. The townspeople were kind and gave generously.

Later, they discovered that this supposedly poor man was really quite well-off. Furious, they called a meeting and decided to forbid any more poor people from entering their town to collect funds.

When Rav Salanter heard about their resolution, he called a second meeting and said, "It wasn't a poor man who swindled you, but a wealthy one. Since that is the case, you should forbid rich people from collecting funds in your town!"

# Buyer Beware

**D**ifferent people have different ways of dealing with their natural suspicions of fund-raisers. I once went to a *baal habayis* to get a donation from him. I had no sooner walked through the door when the man whipped out his checkbook, filled in an amount and told me to write in the name of the institution.

"At least give me two minutes of your time so that I can tell you something about the yeshiva!" I protested. I really feel that if a person is going to give money to an institution, he ought to at least know something about where his money is going.

The man was insistent. "I'd rather not know who you are,

since one always hears *lashon hara* about every institution there is. If you believe it, you'll never give. I prefer to just write a check and let you fill in the name. That way, at least I feel that I'm giving my money *leshem shamayim*."

**A fund-raiser once** went to see a friend of mine to get a donation, but when he entered, he began to have second thoughts. There were already ten people ahead of him in line. The *baal habayis* told him not to worry, since he never turned anyone away. The record to date has been twenty-five fund-raisers in his living room at once!

This friend of mine told me he never turns anyone down, no matter who knocks on his door. The man asking for a donation may be honest or he may be dishonest, but it doesn't make the slightest difference to my friend. He told me that when he was a teenager, people would come to solicit a donation, and he would try to talk his father out of giving to many of them. "You can see the guy is a liar!" he would argue. Or, "Don't give that one anything. You can tell he's a sneak!"

His father maintained that it wasn't up to him to judge who was lying or telling the truth. "Every person will ultimately have to account for what he's done. But I will be judged upstairs the same way I treated others down here. Why lose out on a golden opportunity?"

That's why my friend never turns anyone away.

**A group of people** once came to the Satmar Rebbe suggesting that instead of having the needy come to everyone's door, where sometimes the *baal habayis* isn't home, it would be better to make one central location where the poor could come and get their money.

The Satmar Rebbe answered no because of two reasons: (1) whenever a needy person enters, he brings with him blessing for the home; and (2) if the door doesn't get answered for the needy, it will have to be opened for doctors.

**Many communities** come up with their own ways of dealing with their collective suspicions about fund-raisers. After many years of visiting the same city, I arrived one year only to find that the community had come up with a new system. Anyone coming to the city to solicit funds had to be registered with the local *vaad* (committee) no matter who they were or what institution they represented.

Since I had been going to that city for over twenty years, the members of the community knew me on a personal level. I went to the head of the *vaad* for a donation first, and he gave it to me without any problem whatsoever. Afterward, I asked him for a letter of recommendation.

He looked at me somewhat shocked and asked, "Why would you need one?"

I told him that if every fund-raiser was supposed to get one, then I should have to get one, too. I also wanted to be well prepared in case I found any new potential donors who would want to see the letter.

There are pros and cons to a system like this. The main advantage is that the community feels protected from fraud. When residents see the letter of authorization to collect funds, they feel their contribution is going to a legitimate cause.

For the fund-raiser who is on the up-and-up, the disadvantages are many:

1. It's embarrassing for the fund-raiser.

2. It leaves a lot up to the discretion of the *vaad*. If the *vaad* likes you or your yeshiva, then you could get a better reference; if it doesn't, you're left to their mercy and wind up getting a lot of five-dollar donations.

3. It sometimes takes over an hour to get the form, and then you have to show up only when the *vaad* is in session and hope

they didn't have to run off to some other engagement.

4. Even worse, the *vaad* is usually in its office during "prime time," those hours when any fund-raiser worth his salt should be out on the street making money.

5. You have to represent the type of institution the *vaad* would want the community at large to give to.

The new system didn't affect me too much, since the *baale-batim* already knew me for such a long time. On the other hand, I was just told that this *vaad* found out that 25 percent of the fund-raisers that came to town were out-and-out fakes. It's unfortunate that there are people like that in the field, and it really makes it bad for the good ones.

**It still amazes me** that even though people take all these precautions, there are still some who manage to squeeze their way through. I know of one case where someone comes to the States to raise money because his relative is disabled. He even has papers from the army to prove it. I know this to be true, and the relative doesn't mind, but he does feel that at least he should get some of the money because in reality, people are giving it to him.

**There are cities** that put up fund-raisers during the time they spend in that town. If they run out of space, there's a chain of people that get called to see if they can put someone up. *Baalebatim* don't mind this, and they even look forward to the mitzva. However, it can become hard to do mitzvos like this when your guest disturbs you the whole night making phone calls. Worse is when you get a phone bill for several hundred dollars' worth of calls, made by your guest when he called anywhere and everywhere he could possibly think of.

One *baal habayis* took the phone out of the room so that his guest wouldn't be able to run up such a bill. It didn't help, though, because the fund-raiser came equipped with his own phone, which he plugged in.

**Plenty of suspicions** are completely groundless.

In certain neighborhoods in America, it is virtually impossible to see some of the homes when it is dark outside — and the numbers on them are that much harder to make out. At some homes, the number is written on the house itself, while at others, the number appears on a tree in the front yard. Then again, the number can be on the mailbox, or it might even be on the side of the curb. Sometimes, you can't even see the name of the street!

One evening, after finishing his rounds, a fund-raiser went searching for his host's home. Since he couldn't see where he was going, he used a flashlight to help him locate the house. Unfortunately, a police car passed by and spotted this fellow. After watching him sneak around for a few minutes, they picked him up and brought him down to the station. Worse, the poor man didn't speak any English, so they had to call someone from the religious community to bail him out.

**Sometimes groundless suspicions** can literally ruin a person. You see, people sometimes run to the States to raise money because they've come to the end of the line. Many of them actually work very hard, but no matter what they do, they just can't seem to make ends meet. When they feel they've hit rock bottom, when there are no more corners to cut, they decide that if they're going to survive, they have to give it one last try abroad.

Such was the case with a man who made the fund-raising rounds but still was unsuccessful. Perhaps not enough people believed the truth of his story and didn't want to help him the way he needed to be helped. He felt that the only option left was suicide (which, by the way, is forbidden for a Jew), so he went to the top of a building one day and jumped. At the funeral, one *baal habayis* said to the fund-raiser standing next to him, "Had I known his situation was really that bad, I would have given him a much larger donation."

The fund-raiser standing next to him answered, "My friend, I spoke with you just a few days ago, and my situation is just as bad as his was. Maybe you can help me out?"

The *baal habayis* answered curtly, "So, what do you want from me?"

Sadly, the story is true, and so is the account of the conversation at the funeral. Why does a person have to wait until a poor man commits suicide before he's willing to open his pocket? Isn't the shame of having to knock on doors enough? Isn't that also like suicide? Doesn't it also kill off a part of a person's sense of self-esteem to have to ask others for their help? How far do people have to go?

People ask, "But what if the guy is a crook?" So what? When it comes to other people's motivations, we're all such righteous individuals. Who are we to make judgments about others? If we really had the right kind of faith, and really believed that we will get everything back, wouldn't we push ourselves just a little bit more? If we look at others without suspicion and give what we can, doesn't it mean that heaven will treat us the same way?

**At the same time,** I suggest that serious fund-raisers come prepared. Fund-raising is a venerable profession, and fund-raisers should respect their own profession.

The first rule for every fund-raiser is: never, and I mean never, go into a city without some sort of reference. Always make sure you have the names of a few people who can vouch for your authenticity, your honesty and the existence of your institution.

Second, if possible, always carry with you a list of all your past and present students. Pictures say that you have a nice building, but students say the same thing and more. They tell the public at large what kind of an institution you represent, and they tell a city's residents how many students you have had at your institution from that particular city.

Third, *always* carry a brochure with you. It lends credence to your story, and most people enjoy looking at pictures.

**In addition, I recommend** that every fund-raiser be prepared to answer the following list of commonly asked, legitimate questions:

1. What makes your institution unique? What does your institution do that no other institution does?

2. Where are you located?

3. Who is in charge?

4. Why donate to this particular yeshiva?

5. How does it operate?

6. How long has it been in existence?

7. What has it accomplished?

8. What is the budget of your institution?

9. How many students are there in your institution?

10. Are you tax exempt?

11. What is your position in the institution?

12. Why don't you have a regular job?

13. Why do you represent this specific institution?

If your institution is located in Israel:

14. Are you recognized by the Israeli government?

15. Do you get money from the Israeli government?

16. Are any of your students in the army, and why?

**Once, a man with nine children** and another on the way went canvassing for donations. He was, in fact, collecting for himself, because his large family was crowded into a tiny, two-room apartment. Though he was putting in a full day's work, he just couldn't seem to make a go of it.

When I met him in Cleveland, he showed me a check for fifty dollars that Rabbi Mordechai Gifter had given him. The rabbi had told him to take the check and show it to all the *baalebatim* in Cleveland as evidence that he felt the man's cause was just, and to ask them for their help as well. Unfortunately, he had already finished fund-raising in that city, so the check didn't help.

I met this same man several years later at a wedding in Yerushalayim. He informed me that he had, indeed, made enough money on that trip to buy a larger apartment and that things were going much better for him. Interestingly, after his successful fund-raising trip, various institutions approached him to ask if he would be willing to serve as a fund-raiser for them. His response was that he had only gone to the States to raise money for the apartment, but now that he had it, all he wanted to do was get back to his regular job.

**In the Southeast,** there is a couple that always hosts fund-raisers. All kinds of people stay with them. Some stay for a while, some just for a few days; some speak English, while others only speak Hebrew or Yiddish. Every type of person in every imaginable situation has been under their roof.

Once, they hosted a fund-raiser who seemed strangely removed. For some reason, this couple didn't take a shine to him, so they eventually asked him to leave.

That same day, the husband went to buy a used car from his brother-in-law's dealership. After leaving the lot and getting back on the road, he realized he had no gas in the tank. For some reason, he passed up the first exit and took the second one off of the expressway to find a filling station. The neighborhood wasn't the best, but he didn't feel he had much of a choice in the matter. He went to the first gas station he saw. As he pulled in, who do you think was standing there on the side? The very fund-raiser he had just evicted from his home! The poor fellow was standing there reciting *Tehillim*.

The *baal habayis* asked the fellow what he was doing there, and the man answered, "Well, I had to leave your house, but I had nowhere else to go. I got on a bus and just kept going, until I realized that it didn't make sense to sit on a bus all day long. So I got out and started to say *Tehillim*, hoping that G-d would take care of me."

Needless to say, his former host brought him back to his house.

**Even very respectable people** who go to collect money for others are sometimes suspect. Once, a *rosh yeshiva* in Eretz Yisrael went with another *gabbai tzedaka* to raise money for the poor for Pesach. They came to the home of a certain *baal habayis*, and the man handed them a ten-agura piece (at the time, equal to four cents).

The *rosh yeshiva* immediately turned to the *gabbai tzedaka* and said, "Give him a hundred shekels right away."

The *baal habayis* was taken aback. "Why did you say that?"

The *rosh yeshiva* answered, "Look, you gave me ten agorot, so you must be poor. If you're poor, then I've got to give you money, because I'm out here collecting for people like you."

The *baal habayis* thought a minute, and then said, "The truth of the matter is that I think you are a crook, and that is why I gave you ten agorot. That way, in case you are for real, I won't have missed out on the mitzva of giving charity."

The *rosh yeshiva* then said, "I came here to tell you a story. Since you did give me some money, I'd like to get this story off my chest. There is a woman in the neighborhood who has been abandoned by her husband, and who was left with all the children and all of the debts. She buys her groceries in Mr. So-and-so's grocery. Go and ask him who is putting four hundred dollars a month into his till to pay her bills."

You can be sure that from then on, that *baal habayis* gave

them more than ten agorot!

**Even the greatest tzaddikim** have been called crooks
and turned out of the homes of the wealthy. Reb Nachumke of
Horodna once went to see an attorney to ask for a donation for
the poor. This attorney was Jewish, but it was difficult to see it,
since he was quite assimilated. He was very far from his roots
and was also a big shot in the wider world to boot.

When he saw Reb Nachumke at his door, he humiliated him
by asking, "Who made you into a *gabbai tzedaka*? An old man like
you, stealing from the public? I'm not giving you a single
penny."

Reb Nachumke saw what sort of a person the attorney was,
so he didn't even say a word. He just left.

Several days later, this attorney was convicted of criminal
activity, and the sentence meted out by the gentile court was
very harsh. The attorney made every effort to overturn the judgment. He poured all his money into appeals, but was unsuccessful. He had to be incarcerated for a full two years.

When Reb Nachumke heard about this, he went to visit the
man's wife.

The woman was shattered. She wept before him and said,
"My husband is dead to me for the next two years! I'm like a
widow, and my children are like orphans. All our money has
been thrown away on this court case, and now we're destitute!"

Reb Nachumke tried to console her, and as they spoke, he
gently asked her how much money she needed. She told him she
needed twenty-five rubles a week. He handed her the sum as a
loan, and told her to go on living as she had before.

Every week for the next two years, Reb Nachumke came to
her home and left her twenty-five rubles.

At the end of his jail term, the attorney returned home and
found that the house was the same as he had left it, and his wife
and children looked little the worse for wear.

"How were you able to keep yourself going these past two years?" he asked his wife.

She answered, "The old man who goes collecting for charity gave me twenty-five rubles every week you were gone. If not for him, who knows what would have become of us?"

When the attorney heard her words, he ran to Reb Nachumke with tears in his eyes. He begged the tzaddik's forgiveness for the way he had insulted him, and thanked him for all he had done for his family. He promised to repay the loan from his very first earnings, and vowed to provide generously for the needy.

From that time on, this attorney was a changed man. He returned to his Jewish roots, and his home and hand were always open to the poor.

**Rabbi Shlomo Kluger,** the Maggid of Brod, used to say that *gemilus chassadim* can be done for the living and for the dead. When it comes to helping those in need, people don't rush to give charity or to extend a loan. Yet, when it comes to taking care of funeral arrangements, everyone rushes to help. The reason why this is the case is because people, by nature, want the truth. When a poor man comes to you with an outstretched hand, you're never sure if he's for real or if he's a charlatan. On the other hand, when a man is dead, he's *dead*. There are no two ways about it. That's why, said the *maggid*, caring for the dead is called *chessed shel emes* (true kindness).

**Rabbi Yitzchak of Vorki** used to say that all of a person's character traits, even his bad ones, were given to him so that he could use them for the good. The worst trait of all is not believing in G-d. But what good can a person do with a trait such as that?

Rabbi Yitzchak explained: When a poor person comes to you for help, don't think he ought to have stronger faith and trust in G-d that he will be helped from heaven. Rather, act like a heretic and don't believe that this poor soul has anyone to rely on but you. Then, you'll feel obliged to give generously.

**A certain community** took steps to prevent fraudulent fund-raisers from collecting from its members. Rabbi G. was an outspoken opponent of the plan that required every fund-raiser to first get a letter of approval from a rabbinic committee.

After some time, one of the wealthier members of the community, Mr. N., said he didn't see anything wrong with the way the plan was working.

"Haven't you noticed a sharp drop in the number of fund-raisers coming to town?" Rabbi G. asked him.

"Yes, I have," said the wealthy man.

"Well," said Rabbi G., "that's exactly why I was against it."

**Another time,** a person well on in years came to canvass a U.S. city for donations. He told everyone the funds were going to an orphan who wanted to get married but didn't have any money whatsoever. The orphan wanted to buy an apartment, and since apartments were so expensive in Israel, this would-be benefactor decided to come to the States to raise money for him.

Things were going great for a while, until someone started to ask this octogenarian a few pertinent questions. It turned out that this person was in reality collecting money for himself!

When pressed to tell the truth, the collector said that he didn't see anything wrong with what he was doing, since he was an orphan himself, he really did want to get married, and, yes, he also wanted to buy an apartment for himself. No, he never lied to anyone, but always told the truth.

**As for how to deal with suspicions** when it comes to giving charity, the following story just about sums it up.

The Divrei Chaim of Sanz was renowned for both the manner and the extent of his support of the poor and needy. It was his practice never to keep money in his possession overnight, but to make sure it had been distributed to charity during the day.

Money that came in from his many chassidim was immediately sent to help orphans, widows, *agunos*, wealthy people who had lost all their money, and the poor. If what Reb Chaim received was not enough to meet the day's needs, he would borrow money, using personal items — family silver, down pillows or even his own coat — as collateral.

Reb Chaim continued this practice his entire life. When he reached his later years, his grown children questioned the halachic basis of his generosity.

"Perhaps you could tell us, Father," they asked, "where it states that one must borrow money to give *tzedaka*?"

To this, the Divrei Chaim retorted, "Perhaps you can tell me, my dear children, where there are other children who would take away the one last mitzva their father has?"

"At least check to see if the people asking for money are honest or not," his children suggested.

"If we check up on everyone to see if they deserve to receive from us," the Divrei Chaim answered, "in heaven they will check up on us to see if we deserve to receive from Hashem. Then what will become of us?"

**The Shpolier Zeide** used to give all of his money to the poor, even to poor thieves. When he was asked how he felt justified giving money to known criminals, he would answer, "When it comes time for me to pass on, if I find the gates of mercy locked, I'll send for those same thieves to pick the locks."

**Fund-raisers can be victims** of fraud, too. In the States, as well as in the rest of the world, when a fund-raiser comes to a strange city, he usually has to have someone drive him around, either because he has a poor sense of direction, does not know how to drive, is not familiar with the city or for whatever reason. Many drivers give up their evenings for weeks at a stretch solely for the mitzva. Then again, there are those who are more interested in the easy money that is off the books.

As far as how much they charge for the service, drivers fall into two general categories: (1) those who do it to help supplement their income so that they can support their family; and (2) those who expect to be paid like bankers. Payment to the first group is a legitimate expense in order to help the institution raise funds. The others, as far as I'm concerned, are ripping off the institution.

**Some drivers are paid** a standard fee whether the fund-raiser makes money or not, and some take a percentage of the money collected. Of course, if the driver charges a percentage, he makes sure to take the fund-raiser to the good clientele. If he gets paid by the hour, he can take him to anyone he feels like. In this case, he'll usually go on a fishing expedition as well, trying to find new people to see how much they'll give. The following story, which I heard recently, is about the worst type of driver possible.

"I'm taking you to someone who always gives," the driver would state to his client. "His standard donation isn't much, but if you push, you can get a lot more out of him." In other words, according to this driver, the fund-raiser could get a thousand dollars out of this donor, but only if he pushed hard. "Don't leave his house until you get it," the driver would say, "even if it takes a few hours."

The unsuspecting fund-raiser would climb out of the car and enter the potential donor's home. Quite some time later, he would emerge with a check for a thousand dollars. Since, in this case, the fund-raiser and the driver had agreed in advance that any money collected would be split fifty-fifty, the fund-raiser would give the driver five hundred dollars in cash. The cash was necessary, since, for tax purposes, the driver didn't want to show the extra income.

The whole thing was a scam. When the fund-raiser arrived home, he would find that the check bounced. When finally reached, the donor would invariably say he couldn't come through with the funds since he was strapped for cash.

In the meantime, the driver, who had cut a deal with the fake donor, would give him half of the money, leaving each of them with a clean $250 apiece.

# You *Can* Take It with You

Rabbi Meir of Premishlan was once visited by a poor woman who was at her wits' end. The woman's daughter was about to be married, but the groom was now refusing to marry her until the girl's family added a cow to the dowry.

Reb Meir said, "Dear woman, go to my barn and take my cow."

Later, Reb Meir's wife went into the barn and saw the cow was gone. She came running to tell her husband it was missing.

"Don't worry," he answered calmly. "We'll see that cow again in 120 years."

# You *Can* Take It with You

O nce, when Rav Yechezkel Sarne was on a fund-
raising mission in the United States for the
Slobodka Yeshiva, he arranged a meeting of all of
the yeshiva's benefactors.

One benefactor, who had in fact donated an enormous sum
of money to help the Slobodka Yeshiva move to Hebron in Eretz
Yisrael, later lost all his money. Rav Sarne was hesitant about
inviting him, for he did not want to embarrass him. In the end,
he decided not to invite the man.

Suddenly, in the middle of the meeting, that same benefactor showed up and asked that he be allowed to speak. With great emotion, he said, "Dear brothers, know that wealth is a wheel that turns in the world. Once, I too was a big donor, but the wheel turned on me. Today, I have to scrape together money for bread, and my entire fortune from before is gone completely — except what I gave to the yeshiva to help them move to Eretz Yisrael. Only that merit is left for me, and I would not sell it for all the money in the world.

"From my experience, I advise all of you to give *tzedaka* now! Don't wait, because no one knows what tomorrow will bring. Whatever we do now is what will be with us for all eternity."

His words had a tremendous effect on those present, and the meeting was a great fund-raising success.

**When Rav Simcha Zissel of Kelm** eulogized Rav Yisrael Salanter, he quoted Rav Chaim of Volozhin. "In the future world, the individuals that made up every generation are to be judged by those who were the Torah leaders of their time. This is because angels can't understand what it's like to have an evil impulse. And the tzaddikim of earlier ages can't relate to the trials and tribulations of later eras. So it is left to the tzaddikim of every generation to, later on, judge those who lived in their time."

Once, Rav Chaim Soloveitchik repeated this teaching before a large crowd. An intelligent business man was sitting among them. When he heard what Reb Chaim had to say, he immediately plucked a hundred-ruble note from his pocket and handed it to the rav of Brisk.

"It seems obvious from what you've said that you'll be sitting in judgment upstairs," he said, "so here's a donation for your yeshiva."

**During World War I,** the Chofetz Chaim was living in the town of Smilovitz. When it came time to collect *kimcha* *dePischa* funds, he was told that people weren't donating enough to sustain the poor over Pesach.

The Chofetz Chaim called all the townspeople together to the shul. When everyone was there, he went up to the *bima* and spoke.

"Don't you see that I'm already an old man?" he told them. "Soon I'll have to go up to give a *din vecheshbon*, and one of the questions they'll ask me is if the townspeople of Smilovitz gave charity. How will I answer? If I say that you gave, it would be a lie, and I've never lied. If I say you didn't give charity, that would be *lashon hara*, and that's something I've never spoken."

The Chofetz Chaim didn't get a chance to finish speaking when hundreds of rubles started to rain down from all sides.

**Rav Yisrael of Ruzhin** was once invited to stay at the home of a wealthy man in a certain city. While he was there, all of the townspeople came to see the tzaddik and to receive his blessings. People were coming and going all the time. Since it was the middle of the winter, people were tracking mud all over the fancy flooring of the rich man's salon. The wealthy man was understandably peeved, and made sure to tell everyone, in the strongest language possible, to be more careful.

Rav Yisrael heard what was going on and called his host in to speak with him. "I want to tell you a story," he began. "Once, a poor tax collector lived in a little village. He could barely eke out a living for his wife, six children, his elderly parents, and himself. One year, it was an especially cold winter. The snow fell for weeks on end, and the temperatures dropped to record lows. People shut themselves up inside their homes, not daring to venture out unless absolutely necessary.

"The tax collector wasn't able to make his rounds, and his family went hungry that winter. The month of Adar passed, and the month of Nissan was already upon them. Pesach would be there before you knew it, and the man had no money at all.

"He decided to go to the big city, to see if he could somehow make enough money to get through the holiday. He got into his wagon and set out on his journey. On the way, he met a peasant leading a cow. The tax collector made a deal with the peasant, and bought the cow on credit. He took the cow to market to sell it, and cleared a profit of six rubles. With the money, he bought flour and brought it to the baker. The baker asked him to wait until he finished the other orders, so the man waited. Toward evening, the tax collector's matzos were ready for him. He wrapped them up and headed right home.

"The road home was not the smoothest, and the night was dark indeed. The wagon fell into a ditch, and as much as he tried, the poor man just couldn't get his wagon out of the muddy rut. The tax collector sat down on the side of the road dejected.

"Soon, a rich man passed by with his servants. When he heard cries for help, he sent a servant to go investigate. The servant came back, and reported that he had found a fellow Jew whose wagon was stuck in the mud.

"The rich man ordered his servants to unhitch the team of horses from his own carriage, and use them to help pull the other wagon out. On seeing how haggard and hungry the poor man was, the rich man decided to make sure he got home safely.

"When they reached the tax collector's humble home, the rich man gave him five hundred gold coins. 'Go and prepare for the holiday the way you should, and afterward, open up a winery. Go into business for yourself.' The poor man and his family were overjoyed at their good fortune.

"Years later, the wealthy man passed away and had to stand before the heavenly court to account for his deeds on earth. The man saw groups of angels blacker than pitch standing before him. All of them were shouting at once, 'I was created from this sin that was done in such a place and at such a time.' The noise was deafening. 'Hand him over to us, and we'll bring him to Gehinnom!'

"The man stood there filled with shame. Just then, an angel

whiter than snow came along. The angel called out, 'I was created from a great mitzva this man did on such and such a day at such and such a time. This mitzva should outweigh all of his sins, because one who saves his fellow Jew is considered as if he has saved an entire world, and this man saved a family of ten!'

"The scales were taken out, but the sins still outweighed the mitzva. So the good angel ran to fetch the ten family members to put them on the scale together with the mitzva. It still didn't help. Then the angel went back and brought back the horse and wagon that the man had also saved. Nothing doing. Finally, the angel brought the loads of mud that had filled the ditch, and the mitzva outweighed all the sins!

"This teaches us," concluded Rav Yisrael as he stared straight at his host, "that even the mud that is attached to a mitzva is enough to save a person from Gehinnom."

The wealthy man got the point and stopped complaining about the mud people were tracking into his luxurious home.

**Objects used in a mitzva** not only become a part of a person's heavenly accounting, they even become imbued with sanctity in this world.

Rav Chaim of Sanz, the Divrei Chaim, once came to a certain town. As he walked past one of the houses, he called out that the fragrance of Gan Eden was emanating from it. He felt compelled to enter the house. It was the home of Reb Pesach, the town's charity collector.

Reb Chaim knocked on the door, and Reb Pesach opened it right away. Reb Chaim entered, and sniffed out every corner of the house until he reached the closet.

"Ah!" said Reb Chaim. "This is where the scent of Gan Eden is coming from!"

Reb Chaim asked that the closet be opened up immediately. Reb Pesach was dumbfounded, but who argued with Reb Chaim Sanzer? He opened the closet and emptied it of all its contents.

Worn clothing, rags, and the like tumbled to the floor. Finally, a priest's cassock fell to the ground.

Reb Chaim said again, "The scent of Gan Eden is coming from this! Please, tell me how it came to your hands. What is so special about it?"

Reb Pesach still didn't understand. He thought that Reb Chaim would be angry at him for keeping a garment like that in his home. But he told Reb Chaim the tale.

"I am responsible for collecting money for the communal coffers. I once went out to collect for a good cause, but when I came home, a fellow was waiting there for me. 'Reb Pesach!' he cried. 'I'm in big trouble. My debts are huge, and my creditors are about to pounce on me. If I don't pay them right away, I'm lost.'

"I said to him, 'Why did you come to me so late? I just finished my rounds and gave out all the money. I went to everyone in town to collect. Who can I go to now?'

"The poor man started to cry bitterly. '*Oy!* What *mazel* I've got!'

"I thought to myself, 'I'll try again. The worst that could happen is that I won't succeed. If I do, fine and good. If I don't, at least I tried.'

"I went out to the same people I had gone to earlier and said to them, 'You're right. I was already here this evening. But what can I do? There's a Jew crying in my house right now as I speak. Should he come to you himself and cry to you about his misfortunes?'

"Thank G-d, I managed to collect more money. Everyone gave. Some were hesitant, but even these people gave. When I came home, the man hugged me like a brother. He walked out of my house a happy man.

"Not ten minutes passed before there was another knock on my door. Yet another Jew walked in crying, 'Save me! I'm in such trouble. It's a matter of life and death!'

"I told him straight away, 'My dear friend, I have exhausted all possibilities tonight. What do you want me to do? Should I go out a third time in the same evening? They'll throw me out! Nothing I say or do can possibly help.'

"The man was broken by his troubles and desperate. 'Reb Pesach,' he said, 'if you don't save me, I'm finished. I'll never get on my feet again.'

"I repeated everything I had said before, but he made no move to leave. 'Don't you see that I can't do anything for you?' I said. 'Do you really think that I can go to the same people three times in the same evening? Don't you understand that they'll all throw me out of their homes?'

"But the man just stood there with one thing on his mind.

"We went on this way for a while, until I had a brainstorm. Near my house was an inn where the lowest elements of society used to hang around. They would drink and waste their time playing cards and gambling. I said to myself, 'Why not go there and try your luck? Maybe you'll be able to get something out of them! They might give you a hard time, but you still have to try. You can tell them they're wasting their money on games when a poor Jew needs it more than they can imagine.'

"Leaving the man sitting there, I picked myself up and ran right over to the inn.

"The proprietor was surprised to see me. I had already been there twice that evening to ask him for money.

"'What are you doing here?' he said jovially. 'Don't tell me you need more money!'

"I ignored him and went over to a table. It was hard for me to do it, but I asked the card players for money to help the poor fellow waiting in my house.

"'I've got a deal for you, Reb Pesach,' said one young fellow, grinning. 'Some priest left his cassock here. You put it on, and we'll follow you through the streets of the town playing music. If you do it, I'll give you whatever you need.'

"Fine," I said. But I thought to myself, *Oy vey, what have I gotten myself into? That the town charity collector should pull a prank like this! People will think I've lost my mind!*

"*On the other hand, where else will I find three rubles? I see how welcoming this innkeeper was, and it will probably be the same story everywhere else. I have a Jew in my house who is desperate. Isn't it worth a little shame to save him?*

"I told the group I was willing to do it. I put on the cassock, and they followed me through the streets playing their instruments. People peeked out from every nook and cranny to watch the crazy parade pass by. When they saw that it was me in the lead, they wondered whether or not I had lost my mind. But when we finally finished our grand tour of the town and returned to the tavern, the young ringleader slapped three rubles onto the table and said, 'I made a promise, and I'm keeping it. What's more, I'm throwing the cassock into the deal for you to keep.'

"When I took the garment, I thought, 'This piece of cloth helped me save a Jew. I'm going to keep it.'

When the Divrei Chaim heard this, he was extremely moved.

"You did the right thing!" he told the charity collector. "Make shrouds for yourself out of it. After your 120 years on this earth, you won't need any other shrouds. No destroying angel will be able to touch you when you'll be wrapped in them! Tell your family that they should make sure to bury you in the shrouds made out of this cassock."

And so he did.

Several years after Reb Pesach died, the Polish government decided to run a new road right through the old Jewish cemetery. Naturally, they disinterred all of the bodies in their way so that they could be reburied in a different place. Reb Pesach's body was among those exhumed.

When they opened his grave, they found his entire body

intact — all, that is, except for one foot that was somehow left uncovered by the shrouds.

**In his old age,** the Chofetz Chaim founded the Vaad Hayeshivos, traveling from city to city on behalf of the fledgling organization. As he arrived at the hall of a very big city where he was to speak, he found the building full beyond capacity. There was no room even to enter, so he was lifted on a chair that was passed from hand to hand until he reached the stage. The Chofetz Chaim was already very old and weak and could deliver only a few words. Nonetheless, the entire crowd stood silent, tensely anticipating the words that would come forth from the Kohen Hagadol.

These were his heartfelt words:

"The first question a person will be asked after 120 years is about the mitzva of learning Torah. What will we answer?" At this point, the Chofetz Chaim burst into tears and was unable to continue speaking. All those present began crying together with the *gaon* and *kadosh* of the generation.

Immediately afterward, the crowd filled the collection box of the Vaad Hayeshivos with coins for the rescue of the holy yeshivos.

**In one of the towns** where Rabbi Yom Tov Lipman Heller, the Tosafos Yom Tov, served as rabbi, there lived a very wealthy man named Shimon. Shimon found it impossible to part with his money, no matter how small the amount and no matter what the circumstances.

In this same time, there also lived two ordinary working men, a baker and a butcher, who were paragons of generosity. They were the first to give for any worthy cause, and were known to support thousands of people, some of them secretly.

When Shimon the miser passed away, he had a very small

funeral. The burial society buried him in the section of the cemetery where the lowest of the low were laid to rest.

Soon after the funeral, a strange phenomenon occurred in the town: the baker and the butcher stopped giving charity. The thousands of people they had supported suddenly found themselves in dire straits. Without wasting too much time, they summoned the butcher and baker to the court of the Tosafos Yom Tov.

In front of the great rabbi, the two men admitted that they had stopped distributing funds to charity, but confessed that the money they had given was never their own. All along, they had been getting the money from Shimon the miser! He had sworn them to secrecy out of fear of the admiration and open show of respect people would give him if they knew about his generosity.

After the Tosafos Yom Tov passed away, it was discovered that in his will, he asked to be buried next to Shimon the miser.

**A wicked man took ill** and lost his appetite. When asked what he would like to eat, he finally said, "An egg."

A hard-boiled egg was brought to him, but before he began to eat, a poor man came to him asking for charity. The wicked man told his family to give the egg to the poor person.

Three days later, the wicked man died. Several days after the funeral, he appeared to his son in a dream and told him, "Always give charity! I never did a single good deed during my lifetime other than to give that poor person my egg, but that egg outweighed all the other sins and gained me entrance to the World to Come."

**Two people died** on the same day. One was a Torah scholar, while the other was a public figure whose funeral was attended by many people who came to pay their last respects.

While waiting for the burial to start, the crowd was attacked, and people fled in all directions. Only one person remained in place: a student of the Torah scholar who did not want to leave his rebbe's side.

When the people returned to resume the funerals, a mix-up occurred: the townspeople buried the public figure, while the family of the public figure buried the Torah scholar. The student protested, but no one paid any attention to him.

The student was pained by what he saw as disrespect for his beloved rebbe. He wondered why the public figure was accorded such a distinguished burial.

Later, his rebbe came to him in a dream and said, "Don't feel bad. I will receive my honor in Gan Eden, while the public figure, who was a wicked man, ended up in Gehinnom. The reason for the mix-up in burials is this: I once heard a Torah scholar being embarrassed, and I did not try to defend him. This was my punishment. The public figure once prepared a lavish meal for a city councilman. When the man didn't show up, he gave the whole meal to the poor. For this he was rewarded with a proper burial (*Sanhedrin* 44, Rashi).

**Once a *gevir* gave** a large sum of money for someone's operation. That night he had a dream, and he saw an old man walking with a lot of books. When he asked what was written in the books, he was told these were all of the mitzvos that people did that day.

The rich benefactor asked to see the book on *tzedaka*. When the book was opened, he saw his name in it. However, he was disappointed to see that his name did not head the list. Entered above his name was that of another person who wasn't nearly as wealthy.

When asked why this was so, the old man replied, "You gave a large sum while he didn't, yet with his sum the recipient was able to put together the large sum that he needed. Everyone thought that the smaller sum wasn't worth mentioning, while you already received some of your reward, since because of the large sum that you gave, everyone holds you in high esteem, yourself included.

**Once, when Rav Meir Shapira** of Lublin went to see a wealthy man about a donation, the man said, "I'll give you whatever you need, as long as you give me in exchange your portion in the World to Come."

Rav Meir agreed with one condition. "Fine, except for one piece."

"What piece is that?" asked the man.

"The piece that I will receive for giving you the rest of my heavenly reward just so you will make a generous donation to the yeshiva!"

**Making deals with tzaddikim** over the terms of a donation can backfire.

Reb Nachumke of Horodna once went to a certain rich man for a donation.

The man said to the tzaddik, "I will gladly give you a very large donation, but only on one condition."

"What is the condition?" asked Reb Nachumke.

"That you won't go to Gan Eden without me, and that we shake on it!"

Reb Nachumke agreed to the terms, took the money, and went away with a big smile on his face.

Years went by, and Reb Nachumke's time to leave this world was coming upon him. He called on the rich man one fine day and said, "Please do me a favor. Let's forget about that deal we made."

"That's not the way businessmen make deals," the rich man

replied, indignant. "A deal is a deal!"

"As you wish," said Reb Nachumke casually. "I am now ready to fulfill my part of the agreement. I promised that I wouldn't go to Gan Eden without you, and my time has come. I don't believe our deal said anything about me being under any obligation to wait for your time to arrive, so get ready to go."

The rich man began to tremble with fear, and quickly said, "I forgive you! You can back out of the deal. I won't hold it against you."

**Rav Chaim Soloveitchik** didn't approve of the custom of bequeathing money to charity in a will. "After all," he would say, "once a person dies, he is exempt from doing mitzvos. When a person leaves money to charity in his will, it just means that he missed out on a mitzva he could have done while he was still alive. After all, this is the world of action. The time for doing is now. Later, in the World to Come, a person can enjoy the fruit of his labor, but not the actual mitzva itself."

One of his disciples witnessed Reb Chaim give away all of his money to charity right before he died.

**The Dubno Maggid** said on this subject that he once went for a donation to a certain miserly man who was quite wealthy. The man refused to give anything, saying, "Rabbi, it's enough if I leave my property to charity in my will after my 120 years are up."

The Dubno Maggid responded with a parable.

"A chicken gives very little, just an egg, yet how does the farmer treat his chicken? He takes it into his house and puts it under the table. Even when the chicken gets up on the table and soils it, the farmer doesn't say a thing.

"The pig, on the other hand, gives plenty of meat and oil,

yet we find that the farmer won't let it into the house. What's worse, he may even kick it now and then. Why? Because even though the chicken gives only a little, it needs to stay alive and well to be able to keep on giving.

"The pig may give a lot, but only after it's dead."

**Reb Yankel** was on his way to New York from the Midwest. Since it was a long trip, and driving conditions were deteriorating, Reb Yankel decided to pull off the road and look for a place to spend the night. He pulled into a gas station and asked if there were any motels in the area, and if not, could he spend the night at the gas station. He received a no answer on both counts, and so made his way to a different gas station. He received the same answer there, too. At the third gas station (where, incidentally, they also said no on both counts), the attendant added, "There is an old-age home in the area. Maybe they would put you up for the night."

Yankel found the facility and banged on the door when he got there. After a while, someone finally came to open the door. Yankel explained that he desperately needed a warm place to spend the night. He would even be willing to sleep on the floor. The staff on duty finally relented.

When he met the administrator the following morning, Yankel asked if there were any Jewish houses of worship in the area. The administrator said no. "In fact, the only other Jew I have ever known was a resident here in our facility. He just died this morning."

Yankel realized that Hashem had sent him an opportunity to take care of a *meis mitzva*, and so arranged with the home that he would transfer the body to New York for burial.

At the first cemetery he approached, Yankel was told that they would bury the unknown man only if he would pay three thousand dollars. At the second cemetery, it was the exact same story. Running out of options, Yankel drove to the third cemetery. There he was told that a donor had once given several thousand dollars to the cemetery to cover burial costs in just such cases.

Out of curiosity's sake, they checked their records to see who the donor was.

What do you think? The man who had established the fund was the very same man who was now awaiting burial.

# Tzedaka

"When your brother becomes poor and his means of support fail near you, you should support him — convert or resident — so that he can live with you."

*Vayikra* 25:35

"Should there be a poor person from among your brethren...do not harden your heart or close your hand to [him]. Instead, you should open your hand to him...."

*Devarim* 15:7-8

"The act of tzedaka brings peace, and its effect is tranquility and security forever.

*Yeshaya* 32:17

# Tzedaka

**I** would like to share with you the following quotations from our holy sources and sages. To me, they are inspirational, and some are real eye-openers.

Jews and non-Jews alike are obligated in *chessed*, charity. The destruction of the cities of Sedom and Amora was because the inhabitants did not support the poor. Our sages point out that Jews have an innate tendency to be charitable (*Sanhedrin* 37).

Rebbi Eliezer's students asked him, "What can a person do to be spared the sufferings that will precede the era of Mashiach?"

"Whoever occupies himself with Torah and *chessed* will be spared the birth pangs of that time."

———◈———

Said Rebbi Elazar ben Rebbi Yosi, "Any *chessed* Jews do in this world brings them peace and numerous angels who will advocate on their behalf before their Father in heaven."

———◈———

There are essentially two reasons why many people neglect the mitzva of *tzedaka*. One reason is ignorance of its many applications in life. For example, there is *chessed* for the wealthy and *chessed* for the poor; there is *chessed* for the living and *chessed* for the dead; there is *chessed* a person does with his body and *chessed* he does with his money. Moreover, each of these groupings has a distinct set of laws.

The second reason for the neglect is because many people are unaware of the tremendous power of *chessed* to improve a person's life in all aspects, both in this world and the next.

———◈———

FROM *AHAVAS CHESSED*

## CHAPTER 1

While there is a mitzva to loan money to a wealthy Jew when he is short of cash, the needs of a poor man take precedence. For this reason, the Torah specifically mentions helping a poor person.

If the verse hadn't specified a poor person, a lender would prefer to loan money to a rich man, from whom he could expect favors in return. Also, he would reason that he stood a better chance of getting his money back.

———◈———

## CHAPTER 3

"Tell each righteous man that [his actions] are good, for they shall eat the fruit of their labors" (*Yeshaya* 3:10). This verse teaches us that the *chessed* a man does in this world has the power to cause his repentance to be accepted in heaven, even in cases where strict justice would dictate that such repentance is insufficient compared with the magnitude of his sins.

———

"*Tzedaka* is equal to all the other mitzvos of the Torah combined" (*Baba Basra* 9b).

———

## CHAPTER 5

Rebbe Yehoshua says: "Whoever accustoms himself to giving *tzedaka* merits children who are wise, wealthy and erudite" (*Baba Basra* 9). This means that if a person has not yet had children, through *tzedaka* and *chessed* he will merit to have children.

———

## CHAPTER 6

Said Rav Reuven: "What is the meaning of [the verse] 'and his recompense He shall pay him?' Could it be that when one gives a poor man money, G-d pays him back?

"What it means is this: G-d says, 'This poor man's soul was on the verge of departing from his body due to hunger. You gave him money and restored him to life. I promise to give you back a soul measure for measure. If your son or daughter becomes ill and nears death, I will remember the mitzvos you performed for that poor man, and I will pay you back — a soul for a soul.'"

All this applies when one helps even a simple Jew. However, when one helps a Torah scholar, the merit is much greater. The giver has a share in all the mitzvos this Torah scholar will now go on to do. Also, he merits sitting together with the scholar in the heavenly yeshiva.

———

## CHAPTER 7

When a person fails to engage in *tzedaka* and *chessed*, he becomes penniless, and his fortune will now be spent by others, say our sages.

———◦◦———

## CHAPTER 9

Some people think that *tzedaka* and *chessed* are not even mitzvos. While they consider helping others admirable conduct, they feel there is no actual obligation to do so.

Unfortunately, they have no idea that the obligation — as well as the reward — for acts of *chessed* is the same as that of such familiar mitzvos *d'Oraisa* as sukka, *lulav* and tefillin. Just think for a moment how much we are willing to spend for a pair of tefillin...

———◦◦———

Our sages tell us that more than the rich man does for the poor man [by giving him *tzedaka*], the poor man does for the rich man [by enabling him to fulfill a positive mitzva of the Torah].

———◦◦———

Some people try to get out of giving *tzedaka*, asking, "Am I the only person you could go to? Go to So-and-so. He has more money than I do."

This is nonsense. First of all, who says So-and-so will give the man anything? And even when a poor man has wealthy relatives, writes the Radbaz, if his relatives don't help him, the people of his city are obligated to help him.

Second, once a person is capable of giving *tzedaka*, he becomes obligated to give, and the presence of wealthier people does not remove that obligation.

Sometimes, a person claims, "I once loaned money to someone, and he never paid me back." This is no excuse, because the criminal behavior of one Jew does not automatically transfer the same status to the entire Jewish nation.

If one has the means, knows the person in need of a loan, and trusts him, he is obligated to help. All the more so when collateral is offered.

---

### CHAPTER 12

G-d says to a man, "My son, why don't you learn from your Father in heaven Who sits on His throne of glory? A third of the day He studies Torah, a third of the day He metes out justice, and a third of the day He engages in *tzedaka*, sustaining all creation" (*Tanna D'Vei Eliyahu*).

---

### CHAPTER 13

When a person uses a sum of money to make small loans to the poor, he gains much greater reward than if he were to loan the entire sum at one time. Loaning one time is one mitzva, while by giving smaller sums repeatedly one accumulates many mitzvos.

One should set aside money to be given out little by little. This way, his wife and children can give to the poor when he is busy or sleeping. Also, they will learn from his example, and when they continue in his good ways, Hashem will credit him for having caused this.

Ultimately, everyone has to suffer some monetary losses in life to atone for his sins. Not to lose this money would mean a far worse punishment in Gehinnom, heaven forbid. What point is there in avoiding opportunities to give *tzedaka*, if the same sum would have ended up going to doctors anyway? Our Sages say as much: "A house that is not open to the poor is open to the doctor." Isn't it wiser to avoid all of this from the start by setting aside money for *tzedaka*?

---

## Chapter 14

Though a person who cannot make ends meet is exempt from giving *tzedaka*, we still see that everyone manages to buy a tallis, even though the same exemption would apply there, too. For a tallis, the maximum effort is made, because a Jew wants to fulfill such an obligation.

The same should apply to *tzedaka* as well. A person should put aside money to be loaned out so that he can fulfill this mitzva.

---

## Chapter 16

If a person has no money to give but he encourages someone else to give, he too is rewarded.

---

If a person pledged to give money, but was ultimately unable to do so, he is still rewarded for his verbal declaration. To avoid the problem of making a vow, one should say, "*Bli neder.*"

---

## Chapter 17

While the Gemara states that *chessed* is better than *tzedaka*, there are some aspects in which the reverse is true. For example, when one gives *tzedaka*, he does not receive it back, whereas a loan is returned. The evil inclination uses this detail to convince a person not to "lose money" by giving *tzedaka*. This means that *tzedaka* requires more effort, and the rule is that the greater the effort, the greater the reward.

---

Lately, a new phenomenon has cropped up in which people try to prevent the poor from going from town to town knocking on doors to ask for *tzedaka*, claiming that this actually takes away money from the poor of their own city. Instead, they institute a distribution to the local poor and turn away all outsiders.

This is a grave error. Just because there are poor people in a city, why should one put a complete stop to any other form of *tzedaka*? In *Baba Basra* 7b it states that it is forbidden to erect a door or gate which prevents one from hearing the voices of the poor crying to him from outside.

Moreover, the claim that the poor of one's city must come first applies only to an individual who can give only to one poor person or another. In such cases, the Gemara rules that the poor of one's city come first. However, concerning an entire city, no one has the right to judge who deserves and who does not. Also, when one investigates, one invariably finds that it is the wealthy of the city who push for decrees that place limits on *tzedaka*.

———⊷———

The Rambam writes (*Pirkei Avos* 3) on the verse "everything depends upon the number of one's actions," that giving, say, one thousand dollars one time to one poor person affects a person much less than giving one thousand dollars to one thousand poor people, a dollar at a time.

———⊷———

One does not become poor from giving *tzedaka*.

———⊷———

## CHAPTER 18

A person should immediately set aside money so that he will be prepared for the mitzva of *tzedaka*. In our days as well, the chief function of monetary tithes is to support those engaged in Torah study.

One must also give *maaser* from an inheritance.

———⊷———

If *maaser* has the power to bring wealth, all the more so does it have the power to prevent financial losses. There are, however, many ways in which a person can become poor. Therefore, the Midrash (*"maaser bishvil shelo tis'chaseir"*) hints that even if one of the causes of poverty pertains to a man, if he fulfills the mitzva of tithing, this will balance things out, and, at the very least, he will be saved from losses.

———

According to the Rambam and the Vilna Gaon, a person is obligated to give a fifth of his income to charity.

———

## CHAPTER 21

Providing a person with the means to support himself is a fulfillment of the mitzva of *vehechezakta bo*, literally, "holding a person up" so that he will not need charity.

———

No matter what one's motivations are in giving, money that is given is considered as genuine *tzedaka*. Even if a person loses money, and a poor person finds it, it is considered as *tzedaka*.

———

### FROM CHESHBON HANEFESH

A person thinks that when he's about to die, he'll make a will and tell his children what to do with his money, that they should give it in his name to Torah scholars and various mitzva-related institutions. A few problems can arise, though. First of all, who knows if he will be of sound mind just before his death? One must merit this. Also, some people die suddenly, tragically, heaven forbid. There's also the question of whether the children will fulfill their parent's instructions. Unfortunately, due to our many sins, cases do occur where love of money causes a person to defy both Hashem and his father.

———

The obligation to give *tzedaka* is much greater for a *baal habayis* than it is for a poor person... And the obligation of a wealthy man is greater than that of a *baal habayis*, and for an exceptionally wealthy man the obligation is still greater.

---

In earlier generations, people were careful about their expenditures and bought only essential items, not luxuries. Then, it was possible to fulfill the mitzvos of *tzedaka* and *chessed* with the small amount of money one put aside for it.

Today, though, more money goes to pleasure items like fancy clothes, expensive homes, and servants. This causes *tzedaka* and *chessed* to be viewed as just another luxury, when they are actually a man's success in this world and the next. Due to this faulty reasoning, when a person does give *tzedaka*, he gives far less than what he is able to, as if he himself were a poor man.

It is well-known that *tzedaka* and *chessed* have the power to weaken the Divine attribute of strict justice. Our sages comment on the verse "He shall give you mercy, and He shall have compassion on you" that a person who treats other people kindly is dealt with kindly by G-d. Nowadays, when there are so many diseases and horrible forms of death, we need to increase our acts of *tzedaka* and *chessed* even more. Hopefully, this merit will shield us from the power of strict justice, and mercy will fill the world.

---

## FROM *SHEM OLAM* (CHAPTER 8)

I find it amazing that people look for all kinds of *segulos*, sometimes spending hundreds or thousands of rubles, to be able to have children. It would be better for them to use the *segula* that our sages give, namely that they should engage regularly in *tzedaka*, helping the poor or establishing a free-loan society, and they should persist in this... Many people have done this in our times and were successful.

And even if, *chas veshalom*, it is decreed that a person be childless [meaning, his entire life has gone by, and he did not have children; short of this, no one can prove that such a thing has been decreed upon him, because while there are prayers which are answered right away, other prayers are answered years later, as our sages say], nonetheless, the mitzvos he has done are his progeny....

———

A person's home is blessed through three things: (1) fulfilling the Torah, (2) believing in G-d, and (3) giving a tenth of his profits to charity. Whoever fulfills these three things diligently is surely blessed in this world and the next.

———

## FROM *NIDCHEI YISRAEL* (CHAPTER 35)

The main thing a *baal teshuva* must do is learn Torah, adding on what he can in *Mikra* or Mishna. If he is not a *ben Torah*, let him at least put energy into giving *tzedaka*, and even if he lacks money of his own, let him awaken his fellow man to do *tzedaka* and *chessed* and sustain the poor, all of which help a person merit length of days and atone for his sins...as it states in *Midrash Rabba*: "What should a man do if he deserves a punishment of death from the heavenly court? If he learned to read one page of Torah, let him learn two. If he learned one chapter of Mishna, let him learn two. And if he knows neither *Chumash* nor Mishna, let him become a *gabbai tzedaka*."

———

## FROM *DAVAR BE'ITO* (CHAPTER 20)

Is it logical that a farmer should worry about planting too much seed in his fields? The truth is, the more he plants, the more he reaps, because every seed he plants can grow one hundredfold.

The same holds true for *tzedaka*. Every single penny a man gives to *tzedaka* brings blessings into his home.

Our sages say that in the *asid lavo*, G-d will rebuke every man according to his level. When a person will be asked how he managed the expenses of his home, why he acted like a wealthy man, living beyond his means, his answer will be that there was nothing he could cut back on, that every expense was necessary. Only when it comes to *tzedaka* did he consider his financial position and decide he couldn't do anything. Then he acted like a poor man, not even giving what he was capable of.

---

## FROM *SHIBCHEI RABBEINU HAARI*

There was once a poor man who chased after a *gabbai tzedaka* for a few coins with which to sustain himself. When the poor man didn't get the money, he died on the spot.

Three days later, the *gabbai tzedaka* died, too.

Later, in the days of the Ari, *z"l*, the *gabbai tzedaka* was reincarnated as a boy. The spirit of the poor man also returned to this same boy, and the boy suffered from constant headaches. Finally, his father brought him to the Ari, *z"l*, to see if he could be helped.

The Ari, *z"l*, looked at the boy and told the father not to spend any more money on doctors. They would not help in this case. He then sent for his student, Rabbi Chaim Vital, and instructed him to expel the spirit.

The spirit then told Rabbi Chaim Vital all that had transpired.

---

The reason why charity should go to *Eretz Yisrael* first, possibly even before the poor of your own city, might be because people in *Eretz Yisrael* suffer more, since they must endure most of the hardships that should have affected the Diaspora.

---

The First Temple was destroyed after standing for 410 years. This is hinted to by the words *pe'ah*, *leket*, *shichecha*, which were parts of the harvest left for the poor. The numerical value of the first letter of each word — peh (80), lamed (30), shin (300) — added together equals 410. This alludes to the fact that people in those times were lax in giving charity.

---

When one does *chessed* with the proper intentions, no matter what he does later — giving to the wrong person, giving it to someone who doesn't need it and so forth — the mitzva still counts, because *chessed* overrides any mistake.

---

The Ari, *z"l*, had a *minhag* to stand when giving *tzedaka*.

---

It is good to give charity on *erev Rosh Hashana* because the gematria (*mispar katan*) of *Yitzchak* (yud-tzaddik-chet-kuf), *shofar* (shin-vav-peh-resh) and *tzedaka* (tzaddik, daled, kuf, heh) each equals 19. This merit helps a person to be written in the Book of Life, *sefer hachaim* (heh-chet-yud-yud-mem=19).

---

A poor person or someone raising money for an institution is considered a messenger of G-d. Therefore, anyone who turns his back on the fund-raiser is considered to have insulted G-d.

---

The Rambam says a person has to be more scrupulous with the mitzva of *tzedaka* than with any other positive commandment.

---

FROM _TANCHUMA MISHPATIM_

They learned in the name of Rabbi Meir that when a person is born, his hands are tightly clenched, as if to say, "I possess the whole world." When a person dies, though, his hands are open, as if to say, "I have nothing."

Since this is true, let a person open his hands while still alive to give charity, for that will help him at the time of death.

———⊷———

Ravina was a *gabbai tzedaka* as were Rav Yosef, Rav Papa, Rabbi Akiva, Rabbi Yanai, Rabbi Ami, and Rabbi Pinchas ben Yair.

———⊷———

If a person sees his wealth dwindling, he should give *tzedaka*. That way, he'll have more and more.

———⊷———

If a person wants forgiveness for sins he already committed, he can give more than 20 percent to charity.

———⊷———

Just as when one takes a haircut or a shave, the hair keeps coming back, so too with charity, the more you give, the more keeps coming back.

———⊷———

FROM *MIDRASH VAYIKRA RABBA*

Nothing in this world worse than poverty. Job said to G-d, "I will take upon myself anything You give me, but not poverty."

———⊷———

G-d tests the rich person with wealth to see if he will give enough charity. If he doesn't, he starts to lose his money.

———⊷———

One reason a poor person is called an *ani* (ayin-nun-yud) in *lashon kodesh* is because he is always pursuing money. We can see this by looking at the word for money, *kesef*. *Kesef* is spelled kuf-samech-peh. The letters that precede each of these letters form the word *ani*: ayin comes before peh; nun comes before samech; yud comes before kaf. In a sense, each of these letters is chasing after the letter that follows it in the alef-bet, trying to catch up to it. This is the fate of the poor man, the *ani*, who is always pursuing money.

———

The mitzva of giving *tzedaka* is greater now than in the time of the *Beis Hamikdash*, because back then, there was an abundance of money to go around and fewer poor people. The rich person didn't feel it when he gave charity, and the poor person was able to make the money spread further.

———

Rabbi Chaim Vital would give charity on *erev Sukkos* and said that the mitzva of charity was especially important then.

———

If a person gives charity the proper way, without any blemishes, all his sins are forgiven.

———

A person who gives *tzedaka* need not fear wild animals, for the Divine image is engraved on his forehead, and that rules over all beasts.

———

It is good to give charity before going on a trip.

———

The importance of giving charity on a fast day is alluded to by the word for fast, *taanis*, whose letters can be rearranged to spell *tes la'ani*, give to the poor.

———

When our sages say a person shouldn't give more than 20 percent of his profits to charity, they mean this: If you have already tithed a fifth of your income, you need not go out looking for a poor person to whom to give charity. However, if you already gave a fifth to charity and a poor person comes to you saying he is about to die unless he is helped, you can't exempt yourself from the mitzva, saying you already did it.

——◆◆——

A person who doesn't understand his learning should give charity. That will awaken his heart to understanding the Torah.

——◆◆——

Anything that comes our way unexpectedly is sent by G-d. If a poor person suddenly appears on your doorstep, this, too, is from G-d. You should give *tzedaka*, because G-d sent him for your benefit. Most probably, you needed the merit of that mitzva.

——◆◆——

## FROM *SEFER HAGAON MIVILNA*

G-d sometimes sends poverty to a person to save him from reincarnation and from death in the World to Come (since poverty is already a form of death).

——◆◆——

The Vilna Gaon held that a person should give a fifth of his profits to charity instead of a tenth. If a person gives a tenth, he is guaranteed not to have any losses. However, if he gives a fifth, he is guaranteed wealth.

——◆◆——

## FROM *ME'IL TZEDAKA*

A person should always have money readily available so that he will be able to give even when in the midst of davening.

——◆◆——

When a person makes a profit, he should immediately write it down in a ledger in order to keep a strict accounting of his *maaser*.

Best is to deposit your profits into a checking account specifically for charity. This makes it easy to keep track of your *maaser*.

---

When a person suffers a financial loss, his first impulse is to cut back, not on his expenditures or luxury items but on his charitable donations. This is a big mistake. At first, it seems to work, but in the long run, it will be to his detriment.

---

The *atbash cipher* works by substituting the first letter of the Hebrew alphabet, alef, for the last, tav, the second letter, beis, for the one before the last, shin, and so on. In other words, we reverse the order.

Using *atbash* to replace the letters in the word *tzedaka* (tzadi-daled-kuf-heh) gives us exactly the same letters, in reverse order. We can learn from this that when we give charity, we should turn away from the poor person so as not to embarrass him.

---

One who supports a Torah scholar will be taught and will understand Torah after his death — even if he was a totally unlearned simpleton during his lifetime.

---

If we knew how great this mitzva really is, that it reaches the uppermost parts of the universe, we would pursue it constantly and would never get tired of giving *tzedaka*. This commandment is more stringent then any other positive mitzva in the Torah. It (*tzedaka*) saves us from all kinds of bad diseases, from the judgment of Gehinnom, from natural and unnatural death. It brings you directly into the next world.

---

# Glossary

**Listed here are words** you may or may not be familiar with. Those in italics have not yet made their way into English vernacular and do not appear in English-language dictionaries. Others have become part of contemporary English usage, but for the convenience of readers who have not encountered them previously, they are given here. The definitions are those that best explain the word as it is used in this book.

*a nechtige tahg*: lit., "a yesterday's day." Yiddish vernacular for "forget it"

*Acharonim*: illustrious Torah sages who lived in the period following the publication of the *Shulchan Aruch* (early 16th century)

*agunos*: married women whose husbands are missing, who cannot remarry

*a"h: alav* (f. *aleha*) *hashalom,* may he (she) rest in peace *aliya*: being called up to the Torah; also, elevation of the soul of the deceased

*amud*: stand from which the leader of the prayer service leads the prayers in the synagogue

*apikorsus*: heresy

*asid lavo*: the future to come

*baal/baalas teshuva* (pl. *baalei teshuva*): penitent(s); returnee(s) to Jewish observance

*baal chessed*: philanthropist

*baal habayis* (pl. *baalebatim*): lit., "master of the house." A working man who is head of the household.

*baal tefilla*: cantor

*bachur(im)* or *yeshiva bachur(im)*: yeshiva student(s)

*balebusta(s)*: (Yiddish) capable housewives

*bashert*: predestined spouse

*beis din*: rabbinical court

*beis medrash*: study hall for Torah learning

*beracha(os)*: blessing(s)

*bima*: platform in the synagogue on which the Torah is read

*bnei Torah*: Torah scholars

*chaim*: life

*chap arein*: (Yiddish) to grab an opportunity

*chavrusa*: learning partner

*Chazal*: our sages

*chessed*: loving-kindness

*chessed shel emes*: lit., true kindness; refers to burying the dead

*chiddushim*: original Torah thoughts

*chomesh*: 20 percent of profits given to charity

*chuppa*: wedding canopy

*chutz laaretz*: outside of Eretz Yisrael

chutzpa: (Yiddish) nerve

daven: (Yiddish) pray

*dayan*: religious judge

*derech eretz*: common courtesy

*devar Torah*: a spoken Torah thought

*din Torah*: case brought before a rabbinical court

*din vecheshbon*: a spiritual reckoning

*Eretz Yisrael*: the Land of Israel

*farher*: (Yiddish) to give an oral examination in Gemara

*frum*: religious; pious

*frumkeit*: (Yiddish) religious observance

*gabbai* (*gabbaim*): synagogue attendant(s)

*gabbai tzedaka*: the communal figure responsible for collecting charity money

*gadol hador (pl. gedolei hador* (also *gedolim*): Torah leader(s) of the generation

Gan Eden: the Garden of Eden

*gaon*: genius

Gehinnom: purgatory

*gemach*: free-loan service

*gematria*: numerological value

*gemilus chassadim*: acts of kindness

*gevir(im)*: wealthy person (people)

*gilgul*: reincarnated soul

*gut voch*: have a good week

*hachnasas kalla*: dowering the bride

*hachnasas orchim*: hospitality

*hashgacha* (also, *hashgacha pratis*): Divine providence

*hiddurim*: extra refinements of a mitzva

*Hy"d*: *Hashem yikom damo*, "May G-d avenge their blood";
    used after the name of a person who has died sanctifying
    G-d's name, as in the Holocaust

*kadosh*: holy man

*kapara, kaparos*: atonement(s)

*kavod haTorah*: honor and respect for the Torah

*kedusha*: sanctity

*kehilla*: community

*kiddush Hashem*: sanctification of G-d's name

*kimcha dePischa*: (Aramaic) lit., "flour for Pesach"; providing
    for the festival needs of the poor during Pesach

Knesset: Israeli Parliament

*koach*: power, strength

*kollel*: yeshiva for married students

*landsman*: (Yiddish) a fellow countryman, usually referring
    to someone from the old country

*lashon hara*: slander

*leshem shamayim*: for the sake of heaven

*leshem yichud*: a short prayer focusing one's concentration,
    said before doing a mitzva

*lev*: heart

Maariv: evening prayers

*maaser*: a tithe; 10 percent of profits set aside for charity

*mashgiach*: in a yeshiva, a spiritual supervisor of the students; in commerce, a kashrus supervisor

*masmid*: a Torah scholar who studies with maximum concentration many hours a day

matzos: unleavened bread

mazel: luck

mazel tov: congratulations

*mechalkel chaim bechessed*: [G-d] Who sustains life in loving-kindness

*meis*: dead

*meis mitzva*: a deceased Jew who has no one to bury him

*melave malka*: the post-Shabbos festive meal

mensch: (Yiddish) a well-mannered person

*meshulach(im)*: fund-raiser(s)

*middos*: character traits

mikve: pool for ritual immersion

mila: circumcision

*minhag*: custom

*Mishkan*: the Tabernacle

mitzva: commandment

*moreh horaa*: local halachic authority

*mosad* (*mosdos*): institution(s)

*motzaei*: the night following

*mussar*: ethical rebuke

*neshama (os)*: soul(s)

*nu*: (Yiddish) "so what?"

*oy*: (Yiddish) oh no!

*parnassim*: wealthy and influential community members

*parsa*: about five miles

*peyos*: sidelocks

*pidyon shevuyim*: redeeming captives

*poskim*: halachic decisors

*psak*: ruling

*pushka*: (Yiddish) charity box

*rebbeim*: teachers of Torah

rebbetzin: the wife of a rabbi

*refuah sheleima*: complete recovery

*Rishonim*: illustrious Torah sages who lived in the five centuries prior to the publication of the *Shulchan Aruch* (early 16th century)

*rosh yeshiva*: head of a yeshiva

*rosh kollel*: head of a *kollel*

*rosh mesivta*: head of the yeshiva (*mesivta* is Aramaic for yeshiva)

*ruach hakodesh*: Divine inspiration

*sandak*: person honored with holding the baby on his lap during a bris

schlepp: (Yiddish) to drag or move slowly

*schlepper*: one who schlepps

schmooze: (Yiddish) to chat

*seder*: often used with *learning*, as in *learning seder*; refers to a regularly kept fixed time of Torah study

*sefer, sefarim*: holy book(s)

*sefer Torah*: Torah scroll

*shalom zachor*: a celebration on the first Friday night after a baby boy is born

*shamash*: rabbi's assistant, or caretaker of a synagogue

*shamayim*: heaven

*shana rishona*: the first year of marriage

*Shas*: the Talmud

*she'eilas chalom*: a mystical procedure for receiving Divine insight

*sheva berachos*: seven days of celebration after a wedding

*shidduch*: marriage partner

*shishi*: the sixth aliya (see *aliya* above)

*shiur(im)*: lecture(s)

shiva: the seven-day mourning period after the death of a parent, spouse, sibling, or child

*shomer Shabbos*: Sabbath observant

*shtender*: lectern

*shtetl frum*: Old World religious

*shuk*: market

shul: synagogue

siddur: prayer book

*siyatta diShemaya*: heavenly assistance


*talmid(im)*: student(s)

*talmid chacham*: Torah scholar

*Tehillim*: Psalms

*tlct"a*: (f.) used to distinguish between the dead and the living when both are mentioned in sequence

*tzedaka*: charity

*tzubrochen*: (Yiddish) heartbroken

*vaad*: committee

*vort* (pl. *vertlach*): (Yiddish) short Torah teaching(s)

*yahrtzeit*: Hebrew date of death, commemorated yearly

*yashar ko'ach*: more power to you!

*yichus*: distinguished lineage

*yiddele* (pl.) *yiddelach*: (Yiddish) Jew(s)

*Yiddishkeit*: Judaism

*yiras shamayim*: fear of heaven

Yishuv: the old Jewish community in Jerusalem that preexisted the State of Israel

*zechus*: merit, privilege

*zeidy*: (Yiddish) grandfather

*zuz*: an ancient silver coin